decorate your home **with colour**

decorate your home
with colour

A practical and inspirational guide
with step-by-step projects

Libby Norman

New Holland

First published in 2007 by New Holland Publishers (UK) Ltd
London · Cape Town · Sydney · Auckland
Garfield House, 86-88 Edgware Road
London W2 2EA
United Kingdom
www.newhollandpublishers.com

80 McKenzie Street
Cape Town 8001, South Africa

Level 1, Unit 4, 14 Aquatic Drive
Frenchs Forest, NSW 2086, Australia

218 Lake Road, Northcote
Auckland, New Zealand

ISBN 978 184537 531 7

Senior Editor: **Clare Sayer**
Production: **Hazel Kirkman**
Design: **Lisa Tai**
Picture research: **Lucy Briggs**
Illustration: **Stephen Dew**
Editorial Direction: **Rosemary Wilkinson**

10 9 8 7 6 5 4 3 2 1

Reproduction by Pica Digital PTE Ltd, Singapore
Printed and bound by Times Offset, Malaysia

contents

introduction

Clockwise, from top far right **Red makes a good accent for furniture – particularly when it is linked into the room via patterned curtains or wallpaper. The bold tulip design on the drapes picks out the red of the chair and additional accents of red and orange appear on cushions and vase**

Accessories can become a focal point – be sparing and restrict the colours you choose to create maximum impact

Texture becomes vital with more restricted decorating palettes. Here a mix of elegant linen fabrics adds luxury to a neutral scheme

Pink floral curtains and lime green walls create a contrasting scheme with a distinctly tropical flavour. Although the combination is bold, the addition of white on the furniture, curtains and dado rail ensures the room feels balanced

Simple combinations often have the most impact. Here rich blue walls are matched to crisp white bedlinen

Colour lies at the heart of all successful decorating schemes – whether your taste is for subtle off-white, soft violet or sunshine yellow. It is also one of the quickest ways to improve the atmosphere in your home and gives endless opportunities to add interest through accents and accessories.

And this is where the challenge arises for many decorators. With infinite possibilities offered by colour cards and wallpaper books (along with all those mysterious rules about what goes with what), the process of selecting the right shade can seem baffling. This is where *Decorate Your Home with Colour* comes in. It is a practical and inspirational sourcebook designed to take the stress out of colour scheming. It explains how to narrow down your options and select palettes that are guaranteed to work. But more than that, *Decorate Your Home with Colour* shows you how to approach colour confidently – and use it to create interiors that reflect both your taste and individuality.

Starting with first principles, Understanding Colour describes the simple tools you need to plan a scheme, revealing four tried and trusted colour blending techniques. There are also interior design tricks for making small or awkwardly shaped rooms feel more balanced, plus useful guidance on choosing flooring and planning a new look around existing furniture and fittings.

The three succeeding chapters deal with the subtle and sophisticated end of the colour spectrum, beginning with Black & White and then moving on to the vast

spectrum of Neutrals. You will learn how to choose exactly the right shade and then layer colours to add depth and interest to pale schemes, how to work with the light and proportions of your space – and how to incorporate furniture successfully. A separate chapter is devoted to Rich Neutrals, with guidance on using this contemporary palette of browns and greys to stunning effect. You will also find practical step-by-step advice on preparing walls for a smooth and professional finish, stripping doors and floors and creating painted, stained or grained wood finishes.

If you prefer bolder colours, detailed sections are devoted to each of the major hues on the colour wheel – starting with bold Red, moving round the softer spectrum of Violet, Blue and Green and finishing with the sunny tints of Yellow and Orange. Each chapter shows you the scope available – from mood-setting pastels to dramatic and rich tones. There is guidance on where certain colours work (and where they are best avoided), with expert tips on best partners for accents and accessories.

Each of the ten chapters is illustrated with a wide range of creative treatments for kitchens, bathrooms, bedrooms and living spaces. You will also find 19 practical decorating projects – from matching patterned wallpaper to stencilling, stamping and other clever paint effects. Most projects are easy enough to be completed over a weekend and some can be tackled in under an hour.

Whatever schemes you create for your space – and I hope this book will inspire you to try combinations you had never even considered before – use *Decorate Your Home with Colour* as your guide to the ways in which you can add colour and style to your home.

understanding colour

THE FIRST PRINCIPLES FOR CHOOSING COLOURS ARE SET OUT HERE, ALONG WITH ESSENTIAL INFORMATION ON FLOORS, SOFT FURNISHINGS AND LIGHTING

Colour has the power to transform and brighten our homes – not to mention our day – but before planning major or minor decorating projects it is important to understand the properties each colour contains, and how different shades work together. This first chapter provides essential background information to help you select the right shades, build up a room scheme and use colour confidently on accents and accessories. There are also a few tricks to help you maximise your home's strong points – and minimise problem areas.

Right **This relaxed kitchen diner combines blue walls and floor with accessories in ice cream pink to conjure up a seaside mood**

getting started

We are surrounded by colour every day in nature and in our own homes, and although our eyes can usually spot when two shades work together and when they don't, understanding why can be a more tricky business, especially since colour theory tends to blind us with scientific detail. But successful schemes do not rely on learning complex rules about primary and secondary colours – all you need to get started is a a simple visual tool and a few tried-and-trusted colour-scheming methods.

the colour wheel The best way to understand how colours work together is to refer to the colour wheel. This simple visual tool shows you how to assess the properties of each shade and pick suitable partners for accents and accessories. The wheel illustrates the main colour groups – red, yellow, blue, and so on. Segments that sit side by side are related (harmonious) shades – meaning that they share common pigments. Those at opposite sides of the wheel are contrasting colours meaning they share no common pigments. Each colour segment is represented from its darkest to lightest shade – with darkest at the centre of the wheel and palest at the outer edge. So if you work round the wheel and pick any two shades that sit side by side they will be of similar intensity.

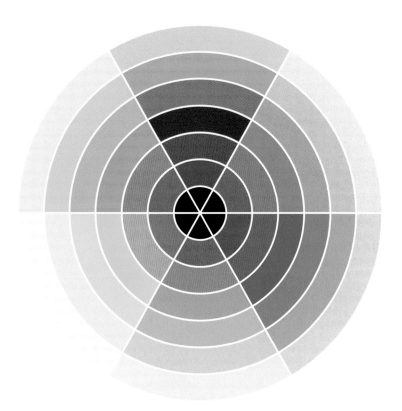

Above **The colour wheel is a simple visual tool which allows you to assess the properties of each shade**

Left **On its own violet can be a cool colour. But partner it with a harmonious shade of deep red and you get a far warmer effect – perfect for adding intimacy to a large bedroom**

The colour wheel on page 10 has black in the centre and white beyond the outer edge of the wheel. These two opposites are dealt with in a separate chapter but bear in mind that there is no such thing as plain black or white – even brilliant white paint has a distinct blue-white sheen.

four ways to blend colours

You can create a variety of effects – from subtle easygoing schemes to daring contrasts, using the colour wheel as your guide. Here are four key methods of creating a colour scheme.

- **Monotone** These are the simplest schemes and because the palette is so restricted they have an elegant contemporary feel. Simply choose shades from one segment of the colour wheel. You can either mix and match two or three adjoining mid to pale shades to create a layered colour effect or stick to one main colour, adding interest with a few well chosen accessories (see Varying the effect with tone, page 12).
- **Harmonious** This is a scheme chosen from adjoining segments of the colour wheel – for instance green and yellow. These are pairings that can be bright or muted but are invariably easy on the eye. If you want to base your scheme around one colour – for instance, yellow – you can add interest by choosing accents from the adjoining segment (in the case of the picture shown above, green and orange).
- **Almost opposite** This offers the key benefit of contrast – a fresh and stimulating environment – but is a little easier on the eye. Choose your main colour and then mix it with shades from the segment to the right or left of its opposite on the colour wheel. Blue and yellow is the classic 'almost opposite' pairing, giving a fresh look to country kitchens or Swedish-style bedrooms.
- **Contrasting** The most daring colourscheming technique, and one that can be bold and stimulating if you choose stronger shades. It is a good choice for children's rooms and high traffic areas such as hallways and contemporary living areas. Popular contrasts are blue and orange and pink and green.

Above left **For this monotone scheme, bold blue walls define a hallway, adding style to the functional grey staircase. The same blue is picked up in the glass pendant lampshade, while the graphic picture on the wall blends blue with accents of grey and white**

Above right **Yellow and green are used to pick out the ceiling angles in this attic bedroom. Choosing similar intensities helps to balance this harmonious scheme and the simple contemporary furniture and white floor stop these bold colours from overpowering the room**

varying the effect with tone

Once you've decided your base shades you need to consider the tonal impression you want – and this is where you can have fun with your colour palette and try out different effects. Below are the main ways to create your palette – but part of the fun of colour mixing is trying out new combinations.

- **Same tone** This is where you partner two or more shades of equal intensity. It is a surefire way of creating a scheme that looks balanced and you can vary the effect by adding brighter accents in furniture or accessories.
- **Colour gradation** For a sophisticated layered effect, mix paler and stronger colours. This works best if you choose from the same or adjoining sectors of the colour wheel. The overall impression is subtle because you are creating light and shade effects. It can be used to add width to narrow hallways or height to low-ceilinged rooms, and works particularly well if you want to use colour to link adjoining living areas.

Left **A bold swathe of red picks out a desk in this contemporary room. Red is continued onto the floor to section off this study zone. It is framed by a soft pink border and the rest of the room is painted white**

- **Tonal contrast** This is the boldest way to use tone and looks most effective if you choose one main colour for walls and then add accents in the contrasting shade. Or pick out one wall for a bold splash of colour and keep it pale in the rest of the room.

Left **This sophisticated wall treatment combines a muted shade of green with a subtle mauve. The bolder blue velvet daybed and ornate gold-framed mirror add a touch of pure glamour**

Above **Dining and living rooms are linked by using soft cream as the main wall colour, with a warmer yellow to define the eating area. This technique adds intimacy to large or open-plan areas**

deciding on a colour

This is the six-million-dollar question for most decorators. Faced with a mountain of wallpaper books and paint charts it can be hard to know where to start. In succeeding chapters we deal in detail with the properties of different colours and the effect they create. Your own personal colour preferences are your best guide, but there are three questions to ask yourself at the outset. These will help you decide on shade and tone – and pick the right look for your room.

- **Atmosphere** Decide if you want this room to be a relaxing or stimulating environment. For a relaxing room consider either using pales/neutrals or going for tones in the blue or deep red/brown spectrum. For a stimulating environment you can afford more daring shades – from lime green to bright orange.
- **Aspect** If your room is flooded with light, then you can choose from across the colour spectrum – including cooler tones of blue, green and lilac. For rooms with restricted daylight or overhanging trees look to colours containing pigments of red and brown.
- **Existing fittings** If you have a carpet, sofa or other dominant fixture that is staying, you need to plan your scheme around it. (See Will it work with the furniture?, page 16, for more advice.)

CREATE A MOOD BOARD

One of the most useful ways to plan a scheme from scratch is to create your own 'mood board'. It allows you the chance to collate the elements that you are considering and then see them side by side. Your mood board can be a large piece of paper or card, or if you prefer a pocket-sized aide that you can carry with you to the shops, use a plain paper notebook or simple folder. Use your mood board to store swatches, paint cards, images of rooms that you love, plus relevant notes such as room and window measurements.

---

how to redefine your space

small rooms Small or awkwardly shaped rooms can be made to feel more spacious if you choose pale and neutral shades. These are what is known as 'receding', which means they have a tendency to create the illusion of more space and light. But this does not mean that stronger colours have no place in rooms with diminuitive proportions – you just need to use them strategically. Here are interior design tricks to try.

- **Small square room** The room can feel as if there is no point of focus. And if it is very small it may feel boxed in. Your best solution is to paint three walls in a pale shade and then create a feature by painting or papering the fourth wall in a stronger toning shade. In bedrooms this looks effective if it is behind the bedhead. In a living room, try creating a feature wall opposite the door – angling furniture so that it faces the bold-coloured wall.

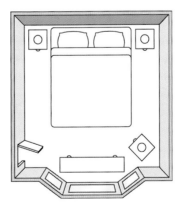

Above left **Square 'boxy' rooms feel larger if you introduce a feature so try painting or papering one wall in a bolder shade. In bedrooms this looks most effective behind the bedhead**

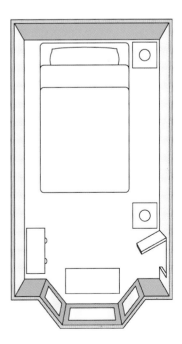

Above right **Small narrow rooms look more balanced if you paint or paper the two longer walls in a different shade. Choose a toning but paler colour to make the walls recede**

- **Long narrow room** The trick here is to minimise the awkward rectangular shape by defining one or both of the longer walls with a contrasting paint or paper – choose a paler shade to make them recede so the room feels more evenly proportioned. If you can, position furniture along the shorter walls to minimise the corridor effect.

large rooms Grand proportions are usually seen as an asset – but they can also feel chilly or soul-less – particularly if the ceiling is very high. This is where darker colours come into their own. They are known as 'advancing', which means they make walls appear closer than they really are.

- **Large square room** The space can feel empty, particularly if it is decorated in pale shades. The solution is to introduce darker colours. But if they are too dramatic the effect can be overpowering. Try combining one wallpapered wall (choose a large-scale design to match the room's proportions) with three painted walls in a toning shade. Alternatively, paint three walls in a deep shade and introduce neutral white or cream to the fourth.
- **Large rectangular room** The proportions are generous but the shape is out of balance. Introduce a rich shade on the two shorter walls. Alternatively, paint or wallpaper one long wall in a rich shade and leave the other three walls neutral. Try angling furniture to create two centres – for instance back-to-back sofas or a study area at one end of the room.

paint v wallpaper

Your choice of paint or wallpaper is a matter of personal taste, but you also need to consider the location you are decorating and the effect you want to create. Here are some watchpoints.

- Paint is generally the safest choice in contemporary settings. If you want to introduce wallpaper, look for bold geometric or abstract floral designs or subtle textured effects. Or hang the wallpaper on just one or two walls to turn it into a focal point.
- Wallpaper is a good option for country-style bedrooms and living areas. Look for small floral designs, stripes or checks. You can add a country feel to kitchens if you look for retro fruit or vegetable designs – particularly effective if you want to create a divide between work and eating areas in a kitchen diner.
- Textured wallpaper is especially robust, making it a practical choice in high-traffic areas such as hallways. Use it in combination with paint – for instance by dividing paint and paper with a dado rail – if you want to create a period feel in a Victorian or Edwardian home.
- Before you choose, consider the practicalities. In damp or steamy environments such as kitchens and bathrooms, choose a specialist kitchen or bathroom paint. If you want wallpaper, look for a design that is described as suitable for these locations – generally it will be a paper containing vinyl or polythene to make it more resistant to damp.

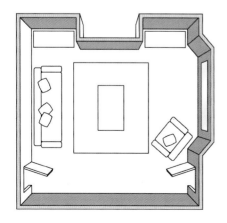

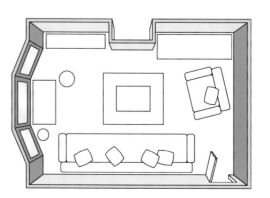

Far left Large square rooms need a point of focus to make them feel more intimate. Either paper one wall in a large-scale design or paint it white/cream and then decorate the other three walls in a richer shade

Left Rebalance large rectangular rooms by decorating shorter walls in a strong colour. Then break up the space by creating two distinct points of focus

other colour influences

Putting paint or paper onto your walls is the most obvious way to introduce colour, but you can create a strong colour impression even if your walls are off white or magnolia. Here are other factors to take into consideration before you start decorating, plus tips to help you accommodate existing fixtures within a new scheme.

flooring Flooring can make or break a room – and since it covers such a large area you can even use it to set the colour mood. If you are installing a new wooden floor or laying carpet or natural flooring, take a swatch with you so you can match it to your paint colour just as you would with curtains or blinds. And if you are redecorating and keeping an existing floor, bring home tester pots or wallpaper swatches so you can ensure a good colour match by testing them in the room. Here are some pointers.

- Wood or laminate floors may appear neutral, but they generally have a distinct colour profile and you need to bear this in mind when you are choosing a wall colour. For instance, pine often has a yellow or orange tinge so you need to choose a wall colour with similar overtones. Pale birch may work best with neutrals that have a blush pink quality and mid or dark oak is generally enhanced by red/brown shades.

- Strong-coloured carpets can easily dominate the room and draw the eye down. This can be a distinct advantage in areas such as hallways, but if you want to stop your carpet from taking centre stage pick a harmonious colour for walls. So a dark red carpet might work best with a neutral that contains pink pigment and a strong blue can be matched to walls in pale dove grey. Sometimes a contrast can work – but it helps your scheme to look balanced if you introduce elements of the wall colour elsewhere in the room with furnishings or accessories.

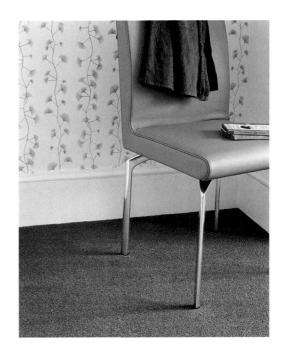

Left **A bold-coloured carpet can work well with neutral walls, but introduce the same colour elsewhere. Here a subtle patterned wallpaper is combined with strong blue carpet. The carpet colour is picked up in furniture to balance the scheme**

Left **Wooden and laminate floors may appear neutral but they have a distinct colour profile so it is important to match walls and soft furnishings carefully. Here a polished pine floor is enhanced with rich green/gold velvet curtains**

- Patterned carpets and rugs are generally best combined with plain walls. You do not have to pick out the main colour in the carpet for your walls but do choose a harmonious shade because strong contrasts will make the room feel too 'busy'. Also bear in mind that if the walls are very pale and the carpet is dark this can make the room appear cold.

will it work with the furniture?

Most schemes have to take into account existing pieces of furniture. Dark leather and wood can be particularly hard to tie into a new decorating plan – particularly if you are trying to lighten the overall look of the room. Your key objective should be to maintain a balanced impression and stop the furniture from dominating. Here are three interior design tricks to try.

- If you have a dark piece of furniture choose an opposite shade for walls and then bring the wall colour into the room via soft furnishings and accessories. You could add new cushions or a throw to break up the expanse of a dark leather sofa, or dress up a table with a runner or table lamp that matches the colour of the walls.
- Paint one wall in a shade that tones in with your largest/most dominant piece of furniture. Now introduce contrasting colours with accessories. These can be used sparingly, but make them dramatic pieces such as bold coloured cushions or a graphic print.
- Pick a strong colour that harmonises with your furniture. For instance, pine works well with shades of yellow or you can pick adjoining shades of green and orange. It is best to keep the walls uniform and accents simple. Add flooring in a similar shade to the furniture to make the scheme feel balanced.

soft furnishings
You don't have to paint or paper your walls in a strong shade to introduce colour. Often soft furnishings can provide all the drama you need – and they give you the chance to alter the mood of a room to suit the seasons, or when your taste changes. They are also an effective way to introduce patterns and textures that reinforce a colourscheme or mood.

Right **A large-scale tulip design makes the window the point of focus in this summery living room. The curtains are combined with plain walls in a soft pink-white shade and a bold red sofa**

Left **One soft brown wall picks out the colour of this leather sofa. Other walls are painted a cooler grey-white, with accessories in shades of bold blue and grey**

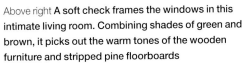
Above right **A soft check frames the windows in this intimate living room. Combining shades of green and brown, it picks out the warm tones of the wooden furniture and stripped pine floorboards**

- If you have large windows, these offer the perfect opportunity to be bold with floorlength curtains. If you choose strong patterns balance this with plain walls. It is also important to match the scale of pattern to the size of the room as a very large print can be overwhelming in a small space.

- Look for more subtle patterns if you want to create an intimate setting – or keep your scheme restrained. Small-scale checks and stripes are a safe bet in both traditional and contemporary rooms, or where you want to keep the overall impression neutral.

- Where wall colours are restricted adding textures gives a sense of depth and warmth to a room. This is particularly important in neutral living rooms and bedrooms, where tactile 'feelgood' materials stop the setting from feeling bland and unwelcoming. Try mixing matt and shiny textures for luxury, or introduce woven or raised fabrics to add a sense of homespun comfort.

CHOOSE THE RIGHT LIGHTING

Lighting is a crucial and often overlooked factor in your room scheme – and if you get it wrong that soft neutral could appear bleached after dark, while the sage green you chose with such care takes on a stark hospital feel. The main culprit in destroying your careful planning is overhead light fittings. Because of their positioning – central to the room casting the light down – they tend to drain colour from a room and produce a harsh and unflattering glare. Try the following solutions.

- Try changing the bulb. Standard bulbs are tungsten, which casts a yellowish light. Introduce tungsten halogen for a stronger and bluer effect that looks closer to daylight.

- Layer the light by introducing light sources at different heights – for instance table lamps and wall-mounted up or down lighters work well in a living room or bedroom, whereas in a kitchen or hallway you will get task lighting minus the glare if you choose recessed halogen ceiling lights.

- Set lighting on a dimmer switch (get a qualified electrician to do this for you) so you can vary the light levels and mood.

- Textured lamp shades are a quick way to soften the effect, particularly if you go for a paper shade, or choose a softly ruched or pin-pricked fabric that filters the light.

- Try a lower bulb wattage. Sometimes all it takes to add warmth to a room is to switch a 60watt bulb to a 40watt.

black & white

OPPOSITES ATTRACT AND YOU CAN CREATE AN ULTRA CONTEMPORARY MOOD USING BLACK AND WHITE – OR GO FOR SOMETHING EQUALLY SOPHISTICATED BUT EASIER ON THE EYE

The ultimate colour contrast, black and white is a surefire combination to define a contemporary home. There are also softer 'faded' combinations of off-white and grey-black that set the same sophisticated mood but create more relaxed living spaces. With such a pared-back palette you can afford to make bold statements with accent colours and it is easy to soften the effect by introducing luxurious textures in soft furnishings. But the most successful black and white schemes involve a 'less is more' approach to accessorising so we have included guidelines to help you tie your scheme together, plus practical advice on preparing your walls to create the smooth finish that is essential for this look.

Right **This 'faded' version of the black and white theme uses soft textures and matt walls to create a relaxing living space**

why choose black and white?

This is a palette of almost puritan simplicity, but choosing black and white gives you the freedom to inject individuality to your room scheme through clever use of accent colours and accessories. It is a chance to create a setting where clean lines and sculptural elements add cutting-edge style. If you prefer you can incorporate more traditional furniture and softer textures for an ambience of understated luxury. This is not a colour combination for busy rooms though – you need to be ruthless about avoiding clutter and careful with the finishes you choose for walls and floors.

Left **With such a restrained palette every detail counts so you need to choose accessory and accent colours that match precisely**

deciding on your look

Forget what you may have been taught, there is no such thing as plain black and white. Even at the deepest end of the spectrum you get inky purple-blacks, subtle tones of steel and rich hints of charcoal. And white has endless permutations of colour, from bright blue-white through to faded chalky or ivory tones. Finding the right pairing is crucial, so you need to start by deciding on the impression you want to create. Here are key decorating styles for black and white.

- **Urban contemporary** This is a smart and streamlined style that partners glossy blacks and bright whites. White is generally the key colour, used on walls and floors with elements of black in furniture and details. It works in open-plan living rooms and smart city-style kitchens, where elements such as granite and chrome add texture and depth.
- **Eastern style** Black and white is the basis of many Eastern-style schemes and here the effect is more natural, with materials such as

Right **Perfect for urban living, black and white creates a light and airy feel. Here walls and floor are in white, with texture provided by the black cord sofa, reflective glass side table and elegant rounded vase**

black-stained bamboo and carved dark wood combined with elements such as rattan, and bronze. Red is usually an accent shade, and there is often subtle woven or printed pattern incorporated into soft furnishings.

- **Faded effects** For a softer version of the black and white palette, use chalky and off-whites in combination with matt blacks and deep greys. This offers the same

sophistication, but without the hard edges and makes it much easier to introduce more traditional elements such as carpet and patterned fabric. Luxurious textures such as wool and linen add comfort in living rooms and bedrooms, while in bathrooms elements such as limestone, granite and chrome create an atmosphere of understated hotel-style luxury.

Above **This Eastern-style hallway combines plain white walls with dramatic black furniture, but the stark contrast is softened through the introduction of shades of beige and deep red on flooring and chair cushions**

introduce stick-on motifs

Tile stickers are a good way to add detailing to plain tiles, and if you choose silver this will add a reflective surface to a black and white scheme. The stickers have a self-adhesive back making them quick to apply. Motifs are best used sparingly – try a border effect around the bath or sink or group them together in a block of four tiles to create a pattern of squares.

① Wash tiles before you start using a mild household detergent and allow to dry.

② Gently peel off the adhesive backing and place the tile stickers lightly in the centre of each tile (you may want to create a guideline with a ruler and pencil).

③ When you are happy with the position of each sticker press down firmly with a dry cloth to secure it in position.

Left **Simple silver tile stickers help to define the area around the bath in a black and white room**

 PRACTICAL TIP

ADD DEFINITION TO PLAIN TILES

Plain white tiles fit perfectly into a black and white scheme if you pick out the grout in black – or charcoal grey for a softer effect. The easiest way to get an even finish is to use a specialist regrouting pen.

1 Wash the tiles thoroughly and ensure the grout is free from grease or mould. Leave to dry for at least one hour.

2 Before removing the lid of the regrouting pen, shake thoroughly to ensure the paint is mixed. Remove the cap and test the pen on an area of kitchen towel.

3 On vertical surfaces work from the bottom up, tilting the pen so the nib faces upwards to ensure a smooth line. If the paint thins, wipe the nib on a kitchen towel. Once the regrouter is applied, wipe excess colour from the surrounding tiles. Leave the tiles to dry for 24 hours.

Above **Black grout lines are an easy way to add interest to an area of plain white tiling**

Tip: If you are tiling a large wall or floor area from scratch and want to introduce black grout lines it will save time if you buy a ready mixed grout colourant in black or grey rather than using a pen.

Above **This bathroom uses texture to create interest, with soft off-white tiles and a natural stone floor in tones of dark charcoal grey. The deep curvaceous bath and oversized chrome showerhead add elements of pure luxury**

try textured wallpaper

Contemporary wallpapers are a great way to introduce subtle pattern and texture to pared back schemes. The same rules apply as for paint, so preparation of walls to ensure a smooth and even surface is essential (see Prepare your walls, below). White-on-white papers create depth and subtle light-and-shade effects and you can use them to create feature walls or hang them throughout to create a more intimate effect in living areas and bedrooms. If you want to introduce a more dramatic impression in a large room look for papers with bold geometric

Right **This simple contemporary living room has sleek modern furniture, but the white-on-white wallpaper featuring raised squares adds texture and depth to the scheme and stops it feeling stark**

prepare your walls

White walls show up every crack and irregularity so it is important to prepare them thoroughly – particularly if you are going for an ultra contemporary scheme. Start by stripping wallpaper, chipping off loose plaster and sanding lightly to see how rigorously you need to fill and repair. Before you start filling, make sure your walls are washed with sugar soap or mild detergent.

- For large cracks and chips use a deep gap filler. This is a thick substance (about the consistency of cream cheese) that comes ready mixed in small tubs. Apply it with a small

trowel, sanding once it is thoroughly dry (usually eight to twelve hours) to create a smooth surface (fig 1). You may need to spot fill once it is dry in areas where the cracks are very deep.

- For hairline cracks, use a paint-on filler. This comes in a tin or tube and is applied with a small brush to smooth out imperfections (fig 2).

Tip: For a really professional finish, apply a base coat of white emulsion after you have filled walls as this will reveal any remaining cracks. You can touch these up with paint-on filler before you apply your second coat of paint. Sanding walls lightly between each coat of paint will also help ensure a smooth and even finish.

fig 1

fig 2

patterning, or a silky textured or fabric finish. (For more information on hanging wallpaper, see Matching bold patterned wallpaper, page 58.)

add wallpaper artwork
If you like the idea of bold patterns but you are not sure you want to use them over an entire wall it is easy and inexpensive to include them as artwork. Bold floral or graphic prints work best for this, but you can also use silk or raised textured fabric or wallpaper if you prefer. If you want to use the design over a small area, simply cut out a square of wallpaper or fabric and insert it into a plain wood frame. This works particularly well if you group two or three 'pictures' together on a wall. Alternatively, go for a bold approach and get an art shop to stretch a square of fabric over a canvas for you for a seamless and lightweight design that can be hung on the wall. Once made, the canvas frame can easily be updated by inserting new fabric to suit your scheme. If you want to use wallpaper, paste this to a square or

rectangle of MDF (a builder's merchant can cut this to size for you). This is heavier than canvas and you will see wallpaper seams but it can be leaned against a wall or attached higher up using a drill, wall plugs and sturdy wood screws. And when you tire of the wallpaper, simply strip the MDF and paste on another design.

Above **A contemporary floral fabric becomes a large-scale and moveable artwork – and you can change the pattern when you tire of the design**

introducing colour to black and white schemes

Black and white can be too severe for some settings and decorating tastes, but it is easy to soften the effect if you introduce additional colours. Here are three variations on the black and white theme, suitable for more traditional bedrooms or living areas.

- **Try mixing it with grey** Adding in tones of soft grey takes the hard edges off black and allows you to work with two or three toning shades. Try mixing a steel grey with warmer tones of blue-grey and lilac for a more feminine setting. It is best to keep walls a neutral off-white or ivory and then introduce black in larger elements such as furniture and flooring.
- **Use brown as your base** Instead of going for black, choose a deep shade of chocolate brown for furniture and combine it with plain white walls. This softens the contrast and also

Left **Rich brown leather sits easily against white and in this living area it has been combined with a deep-pile cream rug for added luxury. The sculptural lines of the Perspex side table and lamp keep the look contemporary**

works well if you introduce shades of beige and cream on woodwork and flooring and then add textures such as suede and wool.

- **Introduce rich neutrals** A less contemporary effect can be achieved if you create a black and white backdrop and then introduce furniture and accessories in rich neutrals. This not only softens the impression, but can be used to add an aged effect – particularly if you introduce retro furniture and eclectic details such as antique gilt or ebony-framed mirrors.

- **Introduce bright accents** Taking black and white as a base – or white and deep grey if you prefer – introduce strong colour elements. For pure drama try red or violet, to lighten the look use turquoise or marine greens. The colours should be restricted to a few key areas of the room, and keep patterns ultra simple. Adding in plenty of white – for instance as a background to a striped or checked fabric – will ensure that the overall colour impression is still black and white.

Left **Grey is the base shade in this contemporary bedroom, but the effect is anything but sombre with blocks of dark pink on side table and curtains and flashes of violet on the bed cover and canopy**

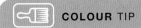 **COLOUR** TIP

GET THE LOOK WITH BLACK ACCESSORIES
If you want the contemporary black and white look but are wary about such a dramatic colour combination, opt for white on walls and floor and then add in black via a few well chosen accessories. This approach works particularly well in kitchens and bathrooms, where it is expensive to change fittings when fashion or your taste changes. Going for a mostly white scheme ensures the room won't date and also gives you the flexibility to add in additional accent colours through accessories if you want to soften the overall effect or ring the changes.

Right **This plain white kitchen is a practical and durable choice, but introducing black accents via furniture and cookware gives it a bold and contemporary edge**

other key elements

Once paint and furniture are in place you can review your scheme. If it feels too stark there are elements you can introduce to create points of focus and add a sense of warmth.

- **Flooring** Introduce comfort to bare tiles or boards. The easiest way to do this is to introduce a rug. Look for luxurious deep-pile wool, natural bamboo, sisal or jute flooring or introduce a traditional kelim or Chinese rug to make a bolder statement. If you prefer plain fitted carpet, choose grey rather than black or the effect will be too sombre. Patterned carpets can look effective in large living areas or halls, but choose stripes or checks rather than florals.

- **Soft furnishings** Texture is the most effective way to soften a black and white scheme. Heavy linens and natural-weave cottons look contemporary and elegant, and you can add more luxurious elements such as cushions in silk or suede, or a knitted woollen throw. With curtains and blinds, choose plain fabrics, or introduce subtle, pinprick, striped or checked patterns. If you go for dark materials, ensure you combine them with light-reflecting

elements such as pale voile panels or a silvered aluminium Venetian blind.

- **Lighting** Use lighting to create areas of light and shade and introduce a sense of warmth. Placing light sources at different heights, for instance by combining wall lights with table lamps, is the most effective way to do this. Pay particular attention to lampshades, introducing textured or cut-out designs that soften and filter the light.

Left **A pinprick design lets in the light and adds a feminine edge to this dark charcoal blind**

Far left **Check carpet is an effective way to add comfort to a large living area or hallway. This pattern is lightened by lines of fawn and grey**

Left **Introduce textured paper or fabric shades to soften and filter the light. This chandelier-style fitting adds a feminine flourish to a black and white scheme**

neutrals

EASYGOING NEUTRALS OFFER A WEALTH OF ELEGANT OPTIONS, ALLOWING YOU TO CREATE SUBTLE TIMELESS EFFECTS OR TAILOR A MORE URBAN AND MINIMALIST SETTING

Neutrals offer a huge range of tones and gradations and they also span the colour wheel – allowing you to create warm or cool effects to suit your setting and your decorating taste. Best of all they offer flexibility, which means you can add bold accents or use clever details to create subtle restful effects. And changing accessories around is the simplest way to keep this palette looking fresh. This chapter outlines the most effective ways to use neutrals and also gives you essential tips for picking a colour that suits your room's aspect and natural light levels. There is also advice on creative treatments for woodwork and guidance on picking details to create a comfortable and luxurious setting.

Right **Neutrals offer a range of subtle colourways,**
which can be used to create warm or cool effects.
Here off-white is combined with accents of fawn
and grey to create a tranquil living room

why choose neutrals?

Neutrals have such obvious virtues that it is no surprise that they are a popular decorating choice for both contemporary and traditional decorating schemes. They make spaces look bigger and maximise natural daylight. Then there is their ability to foster an aura of calm tranquility or urban sophistication depending on the colour you choose and the way you furnish and accessorise the room. Neutrals are chameleon-like too, absorbing and reflecting the colours that surround them. This makes it easy to warm things up a notch for winter simply by introducing curtains or cushions in a richer shade – and then cool things down for summer by switching soft furnishings around again. This may be easy-on-the-eye decorating, but you need to choose your shade with utmost care because what look like miniscule differences on the colour card magnify once you start painting your walls.

WHAT COUNTS AS A NEUTRAL?

A neutral almost always appears at the outer edge of the colour wheel. There are stronger tones of brown and grey which have neutral properties, but these lend themselves to different decorating treatments which we describe in the following chapter.

Neutrals should not be confused with pastels since unlike pastels their key property is their ability to act as background shades, taking on the colour qualities of the objects that surround them.

A neutral is not a 'non colour' though, the pigments contained in the paint or wallpaper will have a distinct aura – be it blush pink or palest yellow – and the same rules apply as with further down the colour wheel even though you are dealing with much subtler degrees of shade and tone. With neutrals it is invariably more effective to opt for a monotone or harmonious palette. If you want to introduce an element of contrast, pick a recognisable colour rather than the opposite neutral.

choosing warm or cool

Faced with so many subtle colours, the best way to narrow down your choice is to consider your room's aspect. Shades with red/pink or yellow/brown pigment in them add warmth, while blue/grey tones generally impart a cooler aura. So if your room is a sunny spot that gets plenty of natural daylight then you can afford to look at the cooler end of the neutral spectrum – in fact this can be a distinct advantage as cooler tones will stop the room from looking bleached in strong sunlight. If you are decorating a room where daylight is restricted then your concern is to add warmth and comfort, so opt for a neutral with hints of yellow, brown or red.

Left **It is easy to add warmth to a neutral setting if you choose from the right segment of the colour wheel and mix and match pale and deeper shades. Here, buttery tones of cream and beige combine with off-white to create a cosy atmosphere in a high-ceilinged room**

deciding on your look

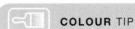

Neutrals are among the most adaptable decorating shades so once you have considered your room's natural light levels, think about the effect you are trying to create. Layers of soft harmonious colours and clever use of texture are perfect for bedrooms or relaxed living areas, whereas bold patterns and stronger accents add a contemporary edge that brings social zones of the home such as the kitchen or dining area to life. Here are key elements for creating contemporary or restful schemes.

contemporary schemes

- Choose a neutral to suit your room's aspect, but to keep the look modern go for more masculine beige/brown or grey tones rather than shades containing pink pigment. Ensure surfaces are prepared and filled thoroughly so

Above **Although this living room is painted in a rich beige, the look is hard-edged, with clean lines on furniture and simple wood and ceramic accessories**

FOUR TIPS FOR PICKING THE RIGHT NEUTRAL Selecting neutrals is notoriously difficult because what look like tiny differences of tone on the colour card magnify once the colour is painted over a large area. The best way to get it right first time is to follow these golden rules.

1   Check the colour in natural rather than artificial light – this may mean taking the colour card outside the store.

2   To see whether it is warm or cool, look down the colour card to the strongest shade. This will give you a clearer idea of the main pigments it contains.

3   Now shortlist a range of neutrals and take tester pots home to try out on your walls. Paint onto large squares of white card or lining paper (it must be white or it will affect the colour of the neutral) and then move these around to test the effect in different lights.

4   Remember the impact of the seasons. You could find your soft rosy white takes on a greenish hue when overhanging trees are in full leaf. Also factor in permanent objects outside the room that may alter the neutral's hue – for instance a neighbour's bright red front door or green fence.

walls look smooth and even and opt for flat water-based finishes for walls such as vinyl matt emulsion. (See Prepare your walls, page 24.)

- Go for bold angular or sculptural lines on furniture and accessories and introduce focal points such as graphic prints and chrome or metal details.

- Add light-reflecting or glossy details, such as silver-framed mirrors, glass tables and metallic ornaments. Dark wood and leather also work well in this setting, particularly if you pick out the same tones in soft furnishings.

- Keep flooring simple – plain wood or laminate floorboards or tiles work best. If you want to add in luxurious elements, look for plain or block-coloured cut or looped pile rugs.

- Pattern can work well on curtains, walls or soft furnishings, but look for abstract or graphic designs – or choose faux animal prints.

Left Large-scale prints work well in contemporary schemes. Here, abstract floral curtains and a graphic striped chair are combined with plain wooden flooring and a deep-pile grey rug

Below This contemporary kitchen-diner combines white cupboards with industrial elements such as the metal-fronted fridge and slimline steel handles. Interest is added through blocks of colour – the blue feature wall and bold red sofa

Large scale patterns generally work best and should be used sparingly – for instance by wallpapering just one wall or by combining patterned drapes with plain painted walls.

- For kitchens choose plain, flat-fronted cupboard doors and add in contemporary details such as metal handles, open shelving and frosted glass cupboards. Worksurfaces can be high-gloss or matt, but choose hard 'industrial' materials such as polished granite, Corian or steel.

restful schemes

- Any neutral can be used to create a restful setting, but your aim should be to create a soft 'blurred' effect with no sharp contrasts or hard edges so look for a colour that will work on both walls and soft furnishings. As a guide, anything in the buttery cream or blush pink range has a naturally restful aura. If you opt for

harder grey- or blue-whites add in softer elements through flooring and soft furnishings.

- Combine textures to add interest and luxury. Suede, wool weaves and crisp cottons all look effective. Mix rough and smooth objects and furnishings to add 'feelgood' tactile surfaces to the room.

- Blend soft pastels with neutrals to create a faded look. This works particularly well in bedrooms and kitchens, where neutral walls can be combined with painted wood for an aged country look. You can mix and match colours, but avoid harsh contrasts and shiny finishes – this is a look that works best if the overall impression remains muted.

- Pattern looks effective used over floors and walls, but go for subtle florals, checks or stripes. Plain or painted wood floors also work well – add rugs in patterned wool or natural materials such as sisal and jute.

Below **Blush walls are combined with a pink floral-patterned carpet for a French country style bedroom. The bureau is painted in a soft grey-green and the bedstead is in faded ivory**

- Keep details simple and homely. Framed prints or heavy-framed mirrors look effective – especially if you mix old and new objects. Introduce soft accent colours such as dove grey, aqua or pale lilac.
- Painted wood in white or cream is the classic choice for a restful Shaker-style kitchen. Combine this with warmer natural elements such as beech worksurfaces and terracotta flooring. Rustic details such as painted tongue-and-groove panelling and a traditional butler's sink combine easily with more modern elements such as steel appliances.

painted floors

Painting your floor is an effective way to introduce soft colour into a neutral scheme, and it's also a good option if you want the bare boards look but your floor is not pristine enough to wax or varnish. Follow the preparation tips below to ensure a professional finish.

Before you start: Fill gaps between boards with wood filler, remove or knock in stray nails and sand thoroughly to create a smooth and splinter-free surface. Sanding will also help to loosen old paint/glue or other finishes. Once the floor is smooth, wash it with sugar soap or mild detergent to ensure it is clean and grease free.

- Woodwash is the quickest and easiest way to transform your floor. The paint is easy to apply, dries quickly and leaves a woodgrain finish. Woodwash is available in a variety of soft colours, you can intensify the colour by applying extra coats. Use a medium-sized brush and remember to paint along the grain of the wood. Follow manufacturer's instructions when it comes to drying time between coats – typically around six hours.

Left Painted floors are a good way to dress up bare boards – and they look particularly effective if skirtings are picked out in the same shade. Use satinwood in high traffic areas such as hallways

- Vinyl matt emulsion is easy to apply, low-odour and dries more quickly than oil-based paints. It creates a matt finish, similar to woodwash but less woodgrain shows through. Use a medium-sized brush and work in quick, even strokes. Allow at least six to eight hours between coats. Finish by applying at least three coats of clear matt varnish to seal the floor.

add aged effects with paint

Even modern furniture can get the traditional finish if you give it a 'distressed' finish using simple painting techniques. This side table is easy to do – but you need to build up your finish with at least two coats of paint so allow plenty of drying time.

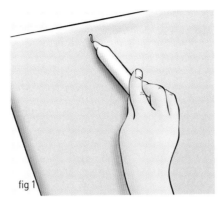

fig 1

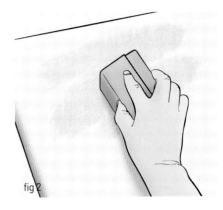

fig 2

① Sand the side table to remove existing paint or varnish and ensure a good painting surface.

② Paint with dark cream/yellow emulsion and leave to dry (around eight hours).

③ Rub the candle over the table, you can do this quite roughly but pay particular attention to edges and areas such as drawerfronts (fig 1).

④ Now paint the table using the paler cream. Work smoothly using long brushstrokes. Leave to dry.

⑤ Sand lightly over the entire surface using the sanding block. The paint should rub off where the candle wax was applied leaving darker paint below (fig 2).

⑥ Once you are happy with the result, seal the table by applying two coats of matt acrylic varnish.

Left **Painting furniture with a distressed finish is an easy technique and the finished result looks especially effective in country-style bedrooms or living areas**

YOU WILL NEED:
- **Sand block and medium-grade sandpaper**
- **Vinyl matt emulsion in dark cream/yellow**
- **Paintbrushes**
- **Household candle**
- **Vinyl matt emulsion in paler cream (one or two shades lighter)**
- **Matt acrylic varnish**

 PRACTICAL TIP

ANTIQUE FINISHES You can experiment with darker shades if you want a more antique finish – for instance starting with brown and then using two shades of cream – just remember to sand between coats and allow at least eight hours drying time. You can add an additional patina of age by rubbing a gold or bronze gilding crayon (available from art supply shops) over edges and drawerfronts.

- Satinwood is an oil-based paint and creates a more robust surface. It has a soft silky-textured finish that makes it easier to remove marks and scuffs. However it does need careful application and a smooth and dust-free floor is essential. For best effect, dilute with white spirit (one part paint to one part white spirit) and paint with a large brush. You will need a minimum of two coats and remember to allow a longer drying time between coats (at least 12 hours). For extra resilience in high-traffic areas such as hallways and playrooms finish with two coats of clear satin varnish.

- Standard paint may not be the best option in areas of very heavy use – or where there are other factors to contend with such as water. In family bathrooms where water splashes may be a particular problem use a heavy-duty floor paint. This should be applied with a medium-sized brush and you need to allow a much longer drying time between coats (typically overnight). Follow manufacturer's instructions carefully.

using carpet to define a room

You can alter the point of focus in a room if you paint walls in a pale neutral and then add colour and pattern through clever use of carpet. This keeps the overall impression in the room pale, but has the added benefit of introducing an element of luxury. This decorating approach doesn't work in all settings, but it is definitely worth considering if you want to add interest and warmth to a large area such as a hallway or draw the eye downwards in a large or lofty-ceilinged living area or study.

- Don't make the contrast between walls and floor too harsh – it is best to pick out similar tones via walls or woodwork or introduce toning details through furniture and accessories.

- Look for a pattern that complements the natural proportions of the room – use large floral or geometric designs only in very large areas or they will overwhelm the space.

- If you have two areas you want to link, consider fitting a carpet with the same base colour but a different pattern. This can be particularly effective on staircases, or if you want to create a 'flow' between hallway and living or dining room.

- In narrow hallways it is usually best to go for a plain carpet, you can add interest by choosing

a design with a border in a different colour – go paler at the edges to add width. Many carpet retailers can custom-design carpet for you, adding a rug effect in the centre of the room or attaching a border in a different colour or pattern to define the edges of a room or staircase.

Above **Subtle hues of fern green create a sophisticated study area. A square-patterned carpet in two shades of fawn adds a welcome burst of warmth and draws the eye down from the high ceiling**

Left You can use the same coloured carpet but vary the pattern if you want to link adjoining areas such as a staircase and hall

Right This hallway is decorated in a fresh off-white, but the two-tone carpet adds warmth and luxury. Clever use of block patterning defines the widest part of the hallway and links it to the staircase

 PRACTICAL TIP

ADD TONGUE-AND-GROOVE PANELLING

Tongue-and-groove panelling looks particularly effective in neutral decorating schemes as it can be used to break up a large wall area. You can either panel the wall to half height – a useful trick if you want to add a feature to hallways – or go to full height in hardworking areas such as kitchens and bathrooms. Have the panelling installed by a joiner, or buy tongue and groove at a builder's merchant. Usually it is sold in packs of 2 m (6½ ft) lengths and you cut it to the required size then fix it to batons using specially designed clamps (get advice from your retailer on the best fixing option for the area you are panelling). Choose your paint with care – a matt or silky finish may be more effective than gloss. Try vinyl matt emulsion sealed with a matt varnish, or use satinwood in areas such as kitchens where you want a surface that can be wiped clean.

Right Wood panelling looks particularly effective in country-style kitchens. Here a soft buttery cream has been used to define a working area, with flooring painted in the same soft shade

colour treatments for woodwork

Brilliant white gloss has a blue-white finish that can easily overpower a subtle neutral scheme. One solution is to paint woodwork in a shade that is a closer match to your walls. You can either go one or two shades lighter so the woodwork recedes and the walls are your main focus, or make the woodwork a point of interest by painting it darker. This looks particularly effective in rooms with ornate skirtings and door surrounds or if you want to frame the area leading into an adjoining room. In areas where there is a lot of woodwork – for instance stairways – it is a good idea to add interest by introducing additional colours. On stairs you could paint the risers a richer shade. This is also a useful safety feature as it helps to define the gap between each tread. Remember to choose a paint suitable for high traffic areas (see page 34).

Above The woodwork becomes the point of focus in this pale neutral study area, with walls painted in a subtle off-white and door frame picked out in a richer caramel shade that matches the bureau

Left This hallway combines soft off-white tongue-and-groove panelling with an area of natural wood further up the stairs. Additional interest is added to the scheme by painting the risers of each stair in a pale aqua green

how to strip wood doors

One of the best ways to add warmth to a neutral setting is to strip the doors. This is best reserved for old pine or hard wood doors, where both the patina of the wood and detailing such as panelled fronts are worth exposing.

fig 1

fig 2

Left **Stripped pine doors look effective in country-style settings and the patina of aged wood warms up neutral schemes**

① First strip the door using a specialist paint and varnish stripper. Apply the paint stripper according to manufacturer's instructions and then scrape off the layers of paint and varnish using a metal scraper. Hold it flat and work gently over a small area to peel the paint off without damaging the wood. If there are several coats of paint to be removed the door may need a second application (fig 1).

② Once the door has had its paint removed, paint on a wood preservative oil to feed the wood and add a soft glossy finish that shows off the grain. Add a tinted oil if you want to darken the colour of the door slightly (fig 2).

DECORATOR'S NOTE

SAFETY ADVICE Follow manufacturer's instructions carefully – wearing gloves, ensuring adequate ventilation and covering the floor area round the door. If you have a lot of doors to tackle it is quicker to have them dipped by a specialist paint removal firm. You pay around £25 per door, but you have to add on the cost of rehanging afterwards – not a job to be tackled yourself unless you are a competent joiner. It is also worth getting doors professionally dipped if you suspect there may be lead paint underneath the gloss.

create the comfort factor

We may associate neutrals with calm living areas and urban minimalism, but they are such an adaptable backdrop that they can work just as effortlessly if your home has more 'stuff' to accommodate. You can even use them to create a bright and stimulating setting in children's bedrooms. Here are three easygoing variations of the classic neutral look.

- **Vintage chic** An open-plan or loft living setting can be decorated in receding neutrals but still have a cosy lived-in feel if you add vintage pieces such as battered leather armchairs, antique rugs and other comfort-zone pieces. The trick here is to decorate with confidence, introducing a variety of colours and textures but never allowing one hue to dominate. Use walls as a gallery and introduce colourful prints, antique-framed mirrors or textile hangings. Go for clever groupings of pictures at eye height or below rather than large or abstract canvases.
- **Boudoir luxury** Bedrooms look particularly effective decorated in neutrals, since these are naturally restful shades. To increase the

comfort factor, add luxurious textures and richer accents, such as chocolate brown, gold and caramel. Introduce faux animal prints, embroidered silk drapes and crisp cotton bedlinen. This is a look that can be adapted for the seasons simply by changing the throw or the colour of the bedlinen.

- **Pattern mixing** Young children respond to bold colours, but you can decorate with neutrals and still provide a vibrant place for play. The key here is to pick a warm tone such as cream or blush pink and then introduce pattern via soft furnishings or a colourful wallpaper border. Mix in stronger hues such as pastel pinks and blues to add depth to the scheme. The best thing about this decorating palette is that you can adapt it as their tastes change – catering to the latest craze by introducing themed bedlinen or a new border.

Above **The walls of this bedroom are painted white, with warmth provided by furnishings in shades of mocha and caramel**

Left **A rich buttery cream provides the backdrop for a riot of pattern. No one shade is allowed to take over and this mix-and-match approach to soft furnishings creates a stimulating setting for play**

Right **A bohemian take on loft living, this eclectic living area is decorated in a soft off-white and assorted picture frames create an unusual feature wall. Battered leather armchairs and a richly patterned antique rug add the comfort factor**

A COSY TAKE ON LOFT LIVING, THIS HIGH-CEILINGED APARTMENT FEATURES AGED LEATHER ARMCHAIRS, A RICHLY PATTERNED ANTIQUE RUG AND A PICTURE GALLERY OF OLD FRAMES DECORATING THE WALLS

rich neutrals

WARM AND INVITING, RICH TONES OF BROWN AND GREY SCORE FOR BOTH STYLE AND COMFORT, ALLOWING YOU TO INTRODUCE MORE OPULENT ELEMENTS INTO YOUR HOME

Earthy tones of brown and grey are the modern take on neutrals – and their growing popularity can be explained, in part, by their ability to give a sophisticated twist to decorating schemes. Like colours at the paler end of the neutral spectrum they have the ability to recede and become a backdrop which you can tailor to your furnishings and taste. But what they also add is light and shade effects – creating a rich and comforting setting that suits both contemporary and traditional homes.

Right **Rich chocolate is a great warm-up colour for cold rooms. Here deep brown furnishings and a textured wallpaper are paired with paler taupe and cream for a sophisticated contemporary living room**

why choose rich neutrals?

Caramel, cappuccino and chocolate brown are instantly appealing (not least for their associations with our favourite pick-me-up foods), and they are surprisingly easy colours to use on their own or in combination. They also offer an earthy warmth that looks particularly effective under cold grey skies – making less of a colour statement than rich red or orange but still adding intimacy to social areas of the home. They blend brilliantly with classic or contemporary dark wood furniture. Grey, on the other hand, adds a cool elegance that harks back to classic country-house decorating or the pared-back sophistication of Swedish Gustavian style. Deeper shades need judicious handling and work best in large rooms, but all greys come to life if you add in other shades. For cooler steelier tones, flashes of gold or orange are perfect partners, while warm dove greys have a grown-up quality that takes the babyish edge off pale pinks and blues.

Above **A pale blue feature wall takes the industrial edge off deep grey kitchen units and helps to make this a social as well as working zone. Softer pale greys are used on tiles, worksurfaces and flooring to add more light to the room**

warm browns

mocha and coffee colours

The starting point for richer neutrals are the coffee colours – creams and beiges with the addition of red, orange or yellow pigment. Like paler neutrals, they work as an effective backdrop but you do get a distinct aura of warmth that lends itself to relaxing living areas and bedrooms. These are not bold statement colours and they make effective partners for mid or dark wood and brown or cream leather, so you can use them with confidence if you are updating a room and keeping existing furniture. Here are tips to help you make these colours work.

Left **Crisp white woodwork helps to lift this restful coffee bedroom. Additional accents of white on the rug and bedlinen balance the scheme**

- White woodwork is a good foil to coffee and mocha walls – highlighting the warm brown tones and adding a crispness that stops your scheme from looking dull. If you prefer a softer alternative, use cream, but avoid anything with strong yellow overtones or the walls will look drab.
- If you want warmth without using beige shades on all four walls, try introducing a soft peach or apricot tone instead. This works well with both cream and earthier brown and creates the illusion of sunshine, making it a good choice for smaller rooms, or where natural daylight is restricted.
- Patterned soft furnishings can be used to impart the same rich neutral effect and give you the chance to keep walls light (useful in small or low ceilinged rooms). Look for designs containing two or three harmonious colours – that way you get a stronger colour impression but have the flexibility to introduce a variety of accents. If you introduce a bold pattern go for plain walls or you will overwhelm the room.
- Another option if you want pale walls is to introduce richer neutral flooring. This treatment lends itself to traditional living and dining rooms and is a useful way of incorporating dark wood furniture into the room. If you opt for carpet or natural flooring you will also add a sense of comfort and warmth underfoot and help to make large rooms feel more intimate.

Below **Blush apricot walls and a creamy coloured sofa are combined with patterned curtains and cushions to create a richer effect. The curtain fabric picks out the warmer orange tones of the cabinet and coffee table as well as the earthier colour of the natural weave rug**

spice and chocolate browns

For a bolder take on rich neutrals, incorporate rich spice and chocolate browns into your decorating plan. These are statement colours and they work best used in combination with other shades. The contemporary way to use them is on a feature wall, allowing you to create a dramatic focal point and then introduce whites or creams on other walls to add a sense of light. In more traditional settings use them to define a masculine study or dining area or cover a large area such as a high-ceilinged hallway. Lift the room by adding in shades of ivory or gold on flooring or accessories or by painting woodwork in soft white or cream.

- For more traditional living areas introduce ginger or cinnamon browns. The addition of orange pigment adds warmth without making the room feel too dark and these spicy tones are perfect partners for leather or suede furniture. Add in light-reflecting accessories in gold, copper or brass to lighten the overall look of the room.

- Dark brown wallpapers work best when they have a silky reflective texture or the pattern incorporates paler shades such as cream or gold. Best used in high-ceilinged rooms, they add intimacy to a hallway or period living room and look particularly effective combined with antique dark wood furniture.

DECORATING TIP

CREATE PERIOD EFFECTS WITH WALLPAPER Rich browns naturally lend themselves to more contemporary settings, but you can use them to create more period effects in bedrooms or living areas if you opt for wallpaper rather than paint.

- Look for classic Victorian or Art Nouveau-style patterns and choose soft faded colours such as caramel, mocha and butterscotch against a white or ivory background.

- It is important to avoid harsh contrasts, so use toning shades for woodwork, flooring and furnishings.

- You can go to town with textures on soft furnishings, adding in soft wool or cashmere cushions and – if you are decorating a bedroom – silky textured throws and eiderdowns.

- Choose colours such as soft peach, silver and gunmetal grey for accessories to add to the luxurious boudoir feel.

Left **Shades of butterscotch or mocha make an elegant backdrop for living rooms**

Right **If you choose a rich neutral wallpaper, add in details in reflective materials such as silver and silk to add to the luxurious effect**

Left This wallpaper has a subtle circular pattern that incorporates shades of ivory and makes an effective foil to the period mahogany side table. With richly textured walls, it is important to introduce blocks of plain colour on flooring, curtains and accessories

Above Rich cinnamon creates a tranquil atmosphere that suits intimate living areas or studies. Here the warm spicy tones of the walls tone in with the ginger-brown leather armchair and gold and bronze coloured accessories

Right This textured paper wall helps to create a focal point in an open-plan living area. The turquoise lamp and dramatic black and white artwork introduce a welcome flash of intense colour

OPULENT AND INVITING, CHOCOLATE BROWN MAKES A GREAT ALTERNATIVE TO RED OR PURPLE IN DINING ROOMS AND WORKS WELL WITH FINE CRYSTAL AND GOLD ACCESSORIES

Left **This intimate dining zone features a rich chocolate backdrop and black tableware and furniture. The feature shelf midway up the wall makes a great display space for a line of candles and gold and glass elements add glamour to the setting**

- Use rich shades of chocolate or cinnamon to create a bold feature wall in an otherwise neutral living space. You can paint the wall (you may need to apply three coats of vinyl matt emulsion for an even finish) or hang a textured or grained wallpaper instead. Deep brown makes a great backdrop for bold artworks and dramatic colours such as turquoise, jade green and burnt orange.

- Brown is a great colour for intimate dining areas – think of this as an updated version of the classic red or purple dining room. The advantage of chocolate shades is that you can keep furniture and tableware ultra-simple and contemporary. Chocolate is also a natural partner for paler neutrals. Add flashes of gold and plenty of glass to reflect the light and add drama to the room.

how to varnish a floor

Rich neutrals lend themselves to stripped floorboards and this is also a good way to add depth and warmth to a room scheme with pale walls. Use tinted varnish for a richer effect.

fig 1

fig 2

fig 3

fig 4

YOU WILL NEED:

- **Hammer**
- **Screwdriver**
- **Medium-grade sandpaper sheets**
- **Hand-held sander**
- **Wood filler**
- **White spirit**
- **Floor varnish (clear or tinted)**

① Hammer in protruding nails and tighten loose screws before sanding (fig 1).

② Using the medium-grade sandpaper, sand along each board with an electric sander to remove varnish, wax or paint. You will find a hand-held sander is easier to manoeuvre and will ensure a better finish, although it takes a little more time to use (fig 2).

③ Fill gaps and holes with a wood filler and sand these smooth once the filler is dry. Allow the dust to settle and then wash with a damp cloth to remove excess sawdust. Then clean the floor with white spirit. Allow to dry (fig 3).

④ Apply floor varnish with a synthetic bristle brush. Leave to dry according to manufacturer's instructions and then apply a second coat if necessary (fig 4).

 PRACTICAL TIP

USING TINTED VARNISH If your floorboards are new (or very pale) you may prefer to apply a tinted floor varnish. These come in a variety of shades ranging from beech effects to antique pine and oak. Ensure you match your floor to your walls. (See page 15 for more advice on matching wood floor colours to walls.)

grey

pale and ice tones

Light greys have an industrial edge that can be harsh and unforgiving when used alone, but combine them with the right colours and they create a sophisticated backdrop that suits both traditional and contemporary settings. They can also be useful partner shades if you want to temper other stronger colours such as blue or pink. Here are two ways to use them.

- **Icy grey** Palest shades are classic cool colours for Swedish (Gustavian) style decorating schemes, where they can be blended with smokier greys and whites. If you go for the subtle effect you need to pay particular attention to paint texture – choosing matt finishes for both walls and woodwork.

Left **Pale grey walls create a neutral backdrop for a study area in a teenager's room. The candy pink furniture adds warmth to the scheme, as does the richer grey tiled floor**

A more easygoing country treatment is to combine ice grey walls with pastel shades of pink, green or blue. This can be particularly effective in bedrooms if you want to take the babyish edge off pale colours. It also gives scope to introduce check or floral patterns.

- **Steel grey** This is a deeper grey with a masculine edge that makes it a good choice in contemporary kitchens and bathrooms but you need to introduce warmer tones and a contrasting crisp white or the overall effect will be dull and muddy. It makes a surprisingly good partner to earthier browns and oranges, or try combining it with deep blues and greens.

warmer greys

Warm greys have an elegance that suits formal decorating schemes. They can be combined with contrasting fawns and deeper blues, or you can go for a layered effect by mixing them with paler greys and introducing shades of cream, aqua and silver.

Left **Steel grey makes a good choice for bathrooms and kitchens, particularly when it is combined with earthy browns, bold oranges and crisp white**

They are best reserved for rooms that receive plenty of natural light, although if you choose a grey with hints of mauve it can be surprisingly forgiving in a north facing room.

- **Dove grey** This has hints of violet that make it a restful choice for bedrooms. Combine grey walls with matt cream or off-white furniture for a Swedish-style scheme – this looks particularly effective against a painted wooden floor. Since the background colour is so muted you can mix small and large-scale patterns such as checks and faded floral designs. Good accent colours include flesh pink, aqua and soft grey-green.

- **Mid grey** Stronger mid greys have a neutral quality that works well with mid and dark blues and beiges/fawns. Combine them with white woodwork and traditional furniture and flooring. You can choose from a wide range of accents (although restrict yourself to two or three to keep the scheme sophisticated), including lilac, rose pink and navy.

Above **Grey creates a sophisticated backdrop in this formal reception room. The steely tones of the walls are warmed up by the fawn and blue patterned carpet and the mid-blue sofa. The white woodwork and roller blind keeps the overall impression simple and maximizes natural light**

Left **This Swedish-style bedroom combines traditional floral wallpaper with a plain painted floor and check curtains. Combining large and small-scale patterns looks effective because background colours are the same**

paint effects with stamps

Stamps are one of the easiest of all paint effects. You can create simple designs with a sponge or half a potato or choose from a huge variety of readymade versions. And stamping is quick and easy to do – perfect if you want to create a feature wall without hanging wallpaper. You can also continue the pattern onto furniture and even fabrics (see tip below).

YOU WILL NEED:

- **Mild household detergent**
- **Small dish**
- **Stamp ink (see tip below)**
- **Small roller or paintbrushes**
- **Ready-made stamp or homemade design**

fig 1

fig 2

① Before you start ensure the surface to be stamped is clean, dry and grease-free. If you are stamping over a painted wall it is a good idea to wash it first with a mild household detergent or weak solution of sugar soap.

② Decide on the pattern you want to create. A larger pattern will look better on a sizeable wall area – as a rough

guide choose something at least 10 cm (4 in) across. Smaller designs are better suited to borders or furniture.

③ Fill a small dish with stamp ink and then dip the roller into the ink and use this to coat the back of the stamp evenly. If you are creating a two-tone design on the back of your stamp, use small paintbrushes instead (fig 1).

④ Press the stamp onto the wall, hold for a few seconds and then lift it off the wall gently. Remember to apply more ink to the stamp for each motif (fig 2).

Right **This simple shape stamped in white ink creates a subtle pattern against dove grey walls. A smaller star motif is continued onto the driftwood-style grey wall cupboard**

DECORATOR'S NOTE

CREATING THEMED WALLS You can mix and match stencils to create a themed wall – for instance lighthouses and sailing ships or apples and pears. This works best if you choose one large and one small stamp.

CREATING PATTERNS
Random patterns often look more effective than regular designs over a large wall area. If you are not confident enough to work by eye, mark the position of each motif using a pencil. Use stamp ink as this is less likely to drip – you can buy varieties for walls and fabric. Versions for fabric need ironing to seal the design so ensure you choose a robust material such as cotton or linen.

A SIMPLE SHAPE STAMPED IN WHITE INK CREATES A SUBTLE PATTERN ON THESE DOVE GREY WALLS

red

THIS STATEMENT COLOUR SETS THE SCENE FOR FEMININE BEDROOMS AND DRAMATIC DINING ROOMS – OR YOU CAN TEMPER IT WITH OTHER SHADES FOR CLASSIC COUNTRY STYLE

From blush pink and bubblegum through to dramatic crimson and rich ochre, colours from the red end of the spectrum are always stimulating. They offer the chance to be bold and contemporary or you can use them in partnership with other colours to create an easygoing atmosphere that works in more traditional settings. These are impact colours – just one wall or even a cushion cover has the power to alter the tone of a room. But use a range of reds together and you dilute their strength, a design trick that can be used to create surprisingly sophisticated effects.

Right **Perfect partners, pale pink and rich red are combined on facing walls to create an elegant setting in this high-ceilinged sitting room. The oversized floral curtains pick out both shades and there are accents of tangerine orange on cushions and vases**

why choose red ?

Pinks and reds are often seen as 'traffic stopping' shades, spelling out romance, passion or drama. But for decorators these are surprisingly adaptable colours. Subtle pale pinks are a tried-and-trusted treatment for bedrooms, but you can also use them to create a retro kitchen or relaxing living room. Meanwhile reds are just as much at home in contemporary dining rooms as they are in rustic farmhouse settings. And if you do not want to paint your walls red or pink, consider using these warm-up colours in partnership with other shades. As accents on rugs and soft furnishings, they can bring a neutral scheme to life or add country-house credentials to muted greens and soft yellows.

Above **Pink is a classic choice for little girls' bedrooms and offers endless scope for colour mixing. Here a subtle gingham check wallpaper is combined with floral bedlinen and curtains and the cheerful striped rug picks up accents of blue, lilac and cerise**

perfect pinks for bedrooms

Paler pinks are a natural choice for country bedrooms, where they impart a soft glow that works brilliantly with traditional painted furniture, voile drapes and embroidered bedlinen. Choose faded peach pinks and the room takes on a sophisticated Art Deco flavour, while stronger hues – usually pinks with the addition of blue – are bright enough to hold their own with lilac and red, making them naturals for vibrant children's rooms. Here are three different bedroom colour schemes to try.

soft rose pink
Easy-on-the-eye decorating, this combines soft ice cream or rose pinks with lashings of white and cream. Texture is important so choose matt paint for walls and furniture to create the right faded feel and combine this with old-fashioned floral wallpaper.

Left **This sophisticated bedroom blends peach pink with shades of fawn, grey and gold. The muted floral wallpaper is combined with crisp white woodwork and a lavish silk bedspread**

Flooring can be plain or painted wood or you can add in deep-pile rugs or fitted carpet for a more luxurious atmosphere.

faded peach Peachy pinks can be among the most sophisticated of colours. Usually they have a hint of fawn or caramel that makes them easy to combine with neutrals or blend with yellows and golds to create a more masculine setting. The overall effect should be muted and good partner shades range from dark ivory to caramel and even smoky grey. Wallpaper generally looks more effective than paint – go for subtle florals or stripes against a peach or fawn background and add in crisp white woodwork to stop the room from looking drab. Silken textures add an Art Deco flavour, while embroidered bedlinen completes the luxurious ambience.

hot pink Turn up the heat and you can create a bold and colourful setting that allows you scope to create a variety of effects. This is pink with plenty of blue in it so it can look cold. The solution is to offset this by combining it with warmer hues of red and lilac. Also mix in plenty of white on woodwork, furniture and bedlinen. For more advice on choosing pinks for rooms with restricted daylight see the Colour Tip below.

 COLOUR TIP

USING PINKS IN NORTH-FACING ROOMS Pink has a reputation for being a cool colour and it does need to be handled with care in rooms that face north or have restricted daylight. Your best solution is to look for shades with plenty of red pigment in them or balance cool and warm pinks (for instance by mixing cerise and rose pink). Include white or cream on patterned wallpaper, woodwork and furniture to keep the overall effect light. Avoid using pink lampshades – white or cream will impart a much softer glow and create a more flattering light. Accent colours should be from the warm end of the spectrum – yellows and golds look particularly effective or you can add in flashes of harmonious red.

Above **A fairytale setting for a little girl, this bedroom blends blue-pink wallpaper with bolder shades of cerise. Accessories in red and lilac help to warm up the room and white curtains and furniture increase the sense of light**

matching bold patterned wallpaper

Matching wallpaper patterns - particularly large-scale floral designs - is not hard provided you follow a few simple rules. Work with a partner, particularly if you need to use a ladder. It is also best to take your time, so cut and hang each length before moving on to the next one.

① Ensure the pattern is the right way up before you start – do not assume the outside end of the roll is the top. Mark the back of each roll before you start to indicate which end is top.

② Measure the length to be wallpapered and allow an extra 50 mm (2 in) at top and bottom. Remember to re-measure the wall at regular intervals, particularly if you have an older home where walls are not always uniform height (fig 1).

③ Decide on the best place to start hanging. This could be a focal point (for instance a fireplace) or the central point of the wall. Never start at a corner if you are hanging a bold design (fig 2).

④ Now cut the first length so that when it is hung and trimmed there will be a complete motif at the top of the wall. Once it is pasted trim top and bottom with sharp scissors (fig 3).

⑤ Before cutting the next length, ensure the pattern matches the previous ones – hanging large-scale patterns means you use more wallpaper but use this technique and you will get a perfect match first time. You can save offcuts for small areas such as above doors or around windows (fig 4).

fig 1

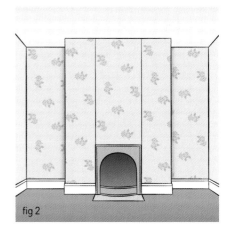

fig 2

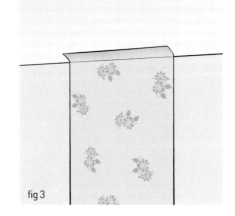

fig 3

fig 4

Far right **Soft pink floral wallpaper creates a romantic backdrop for the ivory-painted bedstead and wardrobe. Wallpaper is used to create a feature wall behind the bed, while remaining walls and woodwork are white**

 PRACTICAL TIP

WALLPAPER BUYER'S GUIDE Always ensure you buy wallpaper with the same batch number as colour printing processes mean tiny colour variations can occur between batches. This may mean buying one or two rolls more than you think you need but these can always be stored in case you need to patch or repair the walls later.

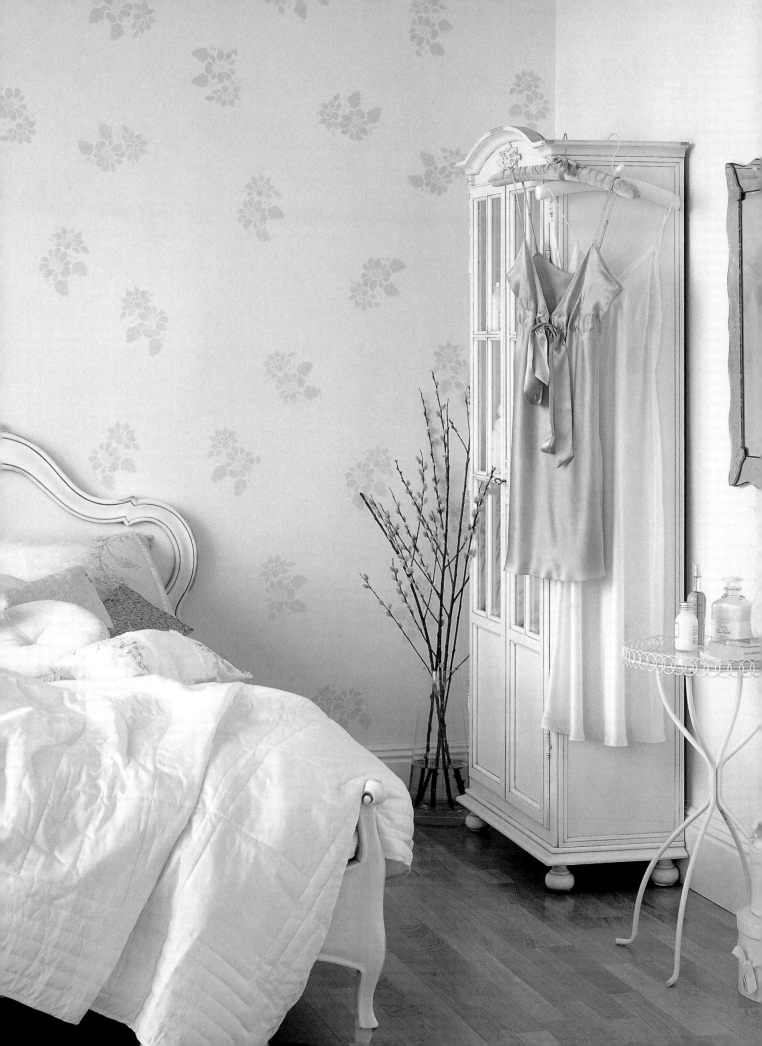

how to use pinks in living areas

Pink has such feminine associations that many people restrict it to bedrooms, but choose the right shade and it can be an effective colour in reception areas – particularly if you want to create a retro 1950s or country-house effect. Even bold cerise can work, provided you balance its intensity with sophisticated greens and browns and add in flashes of crisp white on accents.

retro pink This is a 1950s classic and it can be used in kitchens or living areas provided you mix in lashings of cream (buttery yellow creams are best). Accent colours such as mint green, pale grey and baby blue can work in moderation, and darker tones of lilac and violet also look effective on smaller details.

Left **Pink walls and cream tiles create a retro effect in this kitchen – with country details such as the plate shelf and butler's sink adding to the traditional effect. A simple flower design stencilled above the sink creates a feminine touch that adds style to a working zone**

spray paint a fridge

Use spray paint to decorate a fridge or freezer in a range of colours from pastel pinks to bold reds. The paint is quick to dry, so this is a project that is easy to complete in a day.

YOU WILL NEED:
- **Mild household detergent**
- **Sponge**
- **Dust sheet or newspaper**
- **Masking tape**
- **Aerosol fridge paint**

① First wash the outside of the fridge and ensure it is dust and grease free. Leave to dry. (It is a good idea to empty and switch off the fridge before you start.)

② Cover the area under and around the fridge with a dust sheet or newspaper and ensure the room is well ventilated. Test some paint on an inconspicuous area such as the bottom of the fridge to check it is compatible.

③ Mask off any areas you do not want to paint (for instance fridge handles) with masking tape.

④ Spray lightly and evenly over the surface to be covered, holding the can upright and around 30 cm (12 in) away. You may find it easier to work in strips, from left to right, to ensure the surface is covered evenly.

⑤ Leave to dry as per manufacturers' instructions and apply a second coat if necessary.

Right **Update an old fridge by spray-painting it in pastel pink – the perfect accessory for a 1950s-style kitchen**

Left Tongue-and-groove panelling painted in a soft plaster pink adds an aged flavour to the corner of a country-style sitting room. The effect is deliberately rustic, with soft pink drapes and a battered stone window seat

Below This lavish reception room has accents of green, orange and gold to balance the intensity of the cerise-coloured walls. With such a dramatic colour combination it is important to introduce simpler elements such as natural wood flooring and skirting boards

faded country hues
Pink has country credentials if you choose duskier plaster-pink shades. This is not a colour to be used over a huge area, but it makes a great choice for feature walls or a cosy sitting room, particularly if it is combined with soft ivory, grey or off-white and rustic wooden floorboards. Woodwork on doors and windows should also be painted in softer whites. Go for matt rather than silk paint finishes, the effect you want to create is faded (even weathered) rather than pristine.

sophisticated cerise
Boldest of all the pinks, cerise is best reserved for large or high-ceilinged rooms. Like rich red, it works brilliantly in combination with golds – but also try it with acid greens. You need to maintain a balance by introducing simpler elements such as parquet or varnished wood flooring (choose richer redder tones to balance with the pink). Avoid busy or highly patterned carpets – if you want softness underfoot look for neutral carpet in the fawn/beige spectrum or choose natural flooring in less formal rooms.

using red in your home

It takes courage to apply paint or wallpaper in the boldest shades of red, yet this is a colour that has the ability to bring a room to life, whether you use it on all four walls, create a dramatic feature area or turn up the heat in a neutral room with a few well chosen accents. Here are key ways to use red to add style to your home.

accent colour Red provides an instant lift to neutral schemes, adding a crispness to cream or white furniture and walls. Adding a red rug or runner to a wooden or neutral carpeted floor provides a useful focal point without overwhelming the scheme and you can pick up the red in the rug on accents such as cushions and throws. If you prefer to limit red to smaller accents, use it on details such as cushion covers, sculptural vases candlesticks and small prints but remember to place these carefully. Grouping

Left **Bold red accents such as cranberry glass can introduce a red theme into an otherwise neutral room. Group them together for maximum impact**

COLOUR TIP

CROSSOVER SHADES The most sophisticated pinks of all are the 'crossover' colours – shades which sit somewhere between pink and brown. They have a period quality – reminiscent of the colours you find in 18th-century country houses – which gives them an authentic edge if you are decorating a large room in an older home. They have a naturally muddy quality that absorbs light, making them best for rooms with large windows, high ceilings and plenty of sunshine, but you can use them in bedrooms, living areas or studies without them appearing too feminine. Paler shades work well with greys, silvers and fawns. Richer terracotta pinks can be combined with faded greens and blues or mix them with bare floorboards, antique rugs and dark wood furniture.

Left **This muted pink shade makes a good partner to the soft fawn and russet patterned carpet**

vases, ornaments or prints together on one wall has far more impact than an assortment of individual objects ranged round the room.

furniture and curtains
Red can work well on individual items of furniture, particularly if it picks up a colour found elsewhere in soft furnishings such as curtains. You can include one red chair with neutral or leather furniture, or go for a 'mismatched' feel in more traditional settings by mixing a red chair with a dark coloured sofa. The effect is designed to look casual rather than over-co-ordinated but colours in the furniture can be linked by choosing matching plain or patterned cushions and throws.

wall colour
Red can be too much on all four walls if you have a small or dark room, but it is still a great choice for farmhouse style kitchens – or where you want to warm up a large hall area. You can combine plain painted walls with wallpaper, or introduce additional accent colours such as rich yellow or gold. Choose carefully – richer wine colours are usually easier to live with than zingy orange-reds. If you go for boldly coloured or patterned walls, keep furniture and flooring simple – pale neutrals or plain wood work best. Also ensure adequate light levels in the room by choosing simple curtains and recessed ceiling- or wall-mounted spotlights so the colourscheme does not become too dark.

Above **A classic farmhouse kitchen, this room has red striped wallpaper and accents of gold and red on curtains and china. With such a bold colourscheme, furniture is kept simple with rustic wood units and a dark granite worktop**

red for feature walls

While red can work brilliantly in large farmhouse kitchens, it can be too much for the average sized room if you paint it on all four walls. But if you want to inject intimacy and atmosphere, the solution is to use it on just one or two walls. This works particularly well in dining rooms, where it can be a great mood-setter, particularly if you add candles, red table linen and dramatic gold or silver details.

- Choose neutral colours on the other walls – white, cream or beige/fawn can all work well. Avoid strong overhead lighting – if you use a pendant fitting set this on a dimmer switch and introduce additional layered lighting via wall or standard lamps.
- You may also want to break up the wall area by introducing pictures or wall-hangings – or by adding a shelf for displaying china, candles or ornaments.
- Red wallpaper might be more effective than paint – deep reds often take three coats to go on evenly and with wallpaper you can introduce raised or silky textures to add to the atmosphere and feeling of opulence.
- Red can also work as a feature colour in

Eastern-style living rooms or bedrooms where it looks particularly effective combined with pale woods or mixed in with glossy bamboo and rattan furniture.

Above **This contemporary check wallpaper creates a feature wall behind the bed head in an Eastern-influenced bedroom**

Right **Red becomes a dramatic focal point in an otherwise neutral dining room. Here it is paired with contemporary pale wood furniture and elegant upholstered dining chairs**

create decadent effects with gold

Red is the ultimate colour for creating an intimate atmosphere in your home, which is why it remains such a popular colour for traditional study areas and snug sitting rooms. On its own it has a rich and opulent feel, but add in accents of gold and bronze and you transform it into a 'salon' style setting.

- Combine lavish textures – look for heavy silken fabrics for curtains and plush textures such as velour, faux fur and suede for chairs and cushions. Introduce glamour with gold tassels and trims on cushion covers.
- Details should also be decadent, with gold leaf-decorated boxes and smoked glass vases. If you want to create these details for yourself, you can buy gold leaf in sheets from craft shops (use imitation gold leaf if you want a cheaper alternative) and then attach it to objects such as plain wooden bowls or candlesticks using a special gold leaf glue.
- Try adding gilt effects to furniture or picture frames using a gilding crayon (also available from craft shops) or use a gold stencil paint to pick out details such as the picture rail or panelling on doors.
- Add in lavish details such as gold candles and crystal vases to maximise the sense of light and add an after-dark sparkle.
- Gold also adds a lush quality to paler shades of pink. Try mixing accents of gold with an additional stronger colour such as red or lilac to add warmth and glamour to the room.

Right **Gold is mixed with red to create a 'salon' feel in this luxurious sitting room, with heavy silken drapes and plush textures on chairs**

violet

TRANQUIL OR MOODY, THE VIOLET SPECTRUM INCLUDES THE CALMEST BACKGROUND SHADES – BUT TURN UP THE HEAT AND YOU CAN CREATE THE ULTIMATE OPULENT SETTING

Colours in the violet spectrum range from pale lilac to rich purples – the warmth and intensity they generate depends on the relative quantities of blue and red. Paler shades make a soft alternative to pink in bedrooms, or you can use them to create a bathroom of zen-like tranquillity. More intense shades set the boho mood in intimate dining and living rooms, particularly when they are partnered with rich red or enlivened with flashes of silver or gold. Whatever shade you choose, violet is one of the best choices for adding instant atmosphere and we show you how to blend it with other colours to add depth to your scheme.

Right **A swathe of rich reddish-purple is used to define an internal corridor, emphasising its curvy shape and leading the eye on to the neutral office space beyond**

why choose violet?

Violet can be the happiest of all compromises – blending the warmth of red and the tranquillity of blue. The shade you choose sets the mood – and the temperature – of the room, so pick a bluer shade if you want a cooler effect and a reddish hue if you want added fire. Strength of colour also has an impact on your room; deeper purple tones absorb the light and can make rooms feel sombre or dark unless you add in light reflective details. But as a mood-setting colour, this is almost unbeatable, particularly if you introduce smoky mauve tones into an intimate living area or use this as the basis for an opulent boudoir-style bedroom.

Right **Soft lilac is used to create an aura of tranquillity in this luxurious bathroom. This shade makes a good foil for stronger pinks and turquoises and also blends happily with natural wood**

pale and mid shades

Pale violets and lilacs are perfect backdrops for bedrooms, generating a tranquil atmosphere that works well alongside sugary pinks and blues. Stronger shades make an effective foil for red, or you can go for a layered effect mixing mauves of different intensities to build up the colour intensity.

grey-violet You can create cool almost neutral effects if you pick a pale shade with hints of grey. Woodwork should be crisp white to offset the smoky effect, but you can make the violet appear stronger if you add in accessories in stronger shades of purple. The reverse is true if grey-violet is mixed with pink and red accents. You will find it becomes more of a subtle backdrop, while reducing some of the intensity of the bolder accent colours.

Left **Not as girly as pink, this pretty bedroom is painted in a pale smoky violet and accessorised with stronger pinks, purples and reds**

Above **Lilac walls add a sense of luxury to this bathroom. Floor tiles and fittings are in plain white, while woodwork is painted in a similar shade to the walls**

red-violet Go for a mauve with stronger hints of red if you want to create a setting with more warmth. This is a good option in rooms with restricted sunlight, or where you want to create a more intimate and social atmosphere (for instance living and dining rooms). You can add to the sense of warmth by including elements of red in furniture and accessories

blue-violet Bright blue-tinged shades of violet make a good choice for bathrooms, where they have a bit more warmth than a similar shade of blue, yet still create an aura of calm. If you are going for an intense shade ensure it is matched to plain white bathroom fittings and pick your lighting with care. Ceiling-recessed halogen bulbs will provide a more natural light and stop the wall colour from appearing too flat and blue.

 DECORATOR'S TIP

GET THE LOOK WITH FURNISHINGS If you do not want violet walls it is easy to introduce this warm hue through furniture and details.

- Choose tactile textured materials for furniture such as velvet, velour and suede to provide a luxurious 'feel-good' atmosphere. If you prefer a look you can update more easily, go for neutral textured weave furniture and then add lush details through accessories such as cushions and throws.

- Use shiny or reflective materials for accessories – silk cushions and smoked glass vases add to the opulent atmosphere, as do elements of gold, silver and copper.

- If you want to keep the atmosphere sophisticated, add in neutrals mixing rich mauve and grey-black or partnering a pale violet with a rich shade of fawn. Another option is to go for colour grading, mixing pale shades of violet with much richer and smokier tones.

- Introduce bolder shades on accents – red and blue are harmonious to violet (either side of violet on the colour wheel) and you can also take your pick of bold scarlet, rich wine red, turquoise and jade green.

Above **Violet is a great choice for warming up a neutral setting. Here off white walls and floor are combined with a soft violet sofa in luxurious textured fabric, with paler pink shades used on cushions and footstool**

add a silver foil panel

Adding reflective elements such as this silver panel is an easy way to create a focal point in a painted room – particularly useful if you need to increase light levels. This project takes under an hour and you can vary the effect to suit your scheme. If you choose a bold colour such as violet it is important to add elements that lighten the overall look of the room. This simple stick-on foil square design is used to create a panel in this contemporary dining room. A series of squares creates a window effect, but a border or random grouping would work equally well.

Above Silver foil shapes are a quick way to transform a room. Here they have been used to create a panel behind a dining table, adding interest to a rich violet feature wall

DECORATOR'S NOTE

CHOOSING YOUR DESIGN Self-adhesive shapes are available in a wide range of colours and sizes, but choose a bold design if you are working against a vivid colour such as violet and then pick out the same tones in accessories.

Tip: You can create a similar effect using stencils and stamps combined with a metallic paint or ink.

YOU WILL NEED:

- **Foil self-adhesive motifs in your chosen design**
- **Pencil**
- **Ruler**
- **Spirit level**
- **Dry cloth**

① First ensure that your walls are clean and free from dust and grease. If they are freshly painted ensure they are thoroughly dry (at least 24 hours) before you create this effect.

② Decide on the pattern you want to create, then make pencil marks as a guide to the position of each foil square, marking diagonal corners to ensure they are placed straight. It is a good idea to use a ruler and spirit level to ensure you line them up correctly.

③ Carefully peel off the adhesive backing according to manufacturer's instructions and position each motif lightly (at this stage they can still be moved). Stand back and check the position again before fixing the motifs in place using the cloth. To do this press down firmly and evenly, smoothing out any pockets of air.

pattern mixing

Violet is one of the most adaptable colours, blending easily with blues, reds, greens and yellows. Choosing patterned wallpaper or soft furnishings helps to soften violet's blue overtones – a particularly useful technique if you are introducing it into a room that faces north, or where natural daylight is restricted.

- If you choose a blue-violet, make sure it includes plenty of white within the pattern and opt for curtains or blinds in lightweight material so you maximise natural daylight. Add crisp white to ceiling and woodwork to further increase the sense of light.
- Mix bold pictorial patterns with stripes and checks for a cheerful effect that is ideal for girls' bedrooms. Look for candy or ice cream shades and consider combining a bold border and curtains with a plainer wallpaper in a toning shade.
- For a more intense and altogether more grown-up effect, choose a textured wallpaper with elements of silvery blue or pink in its design. This looks particularly effective in

boudoir style bedrooms, where a bold floral or graphic design can be used to create a feature wall. Combine this with white walls or choose a silvery grey and add in accessories in silver and clear or smoked glass.

Above **Houses in shades of pink, yellow and blue decorate this curtain. The same pattern is used for a wide border framing the window**

CREATE A FEATURE ALCOVE The usual treatment for shelves and alcoves is to paint them white, but if you pick the area out in dark paint you can create a striking feature. The effect is maximised by highlighting the alcove in the same shade as a facing wall, and then papering around the alcove using a bold floral design. This requires a steady hand as you will need to trim the paper exactly so that you leave a straight edge around all four sides of the alcove. Measure up your paper as normal and paper down to the top and sides of the alcove then trim into the alcove using a craft or Stanley knife to ensure a really straight edge. You can reverse the technique if you like – papering inside the alcove to match a facing wall and then painting the wall around it.

Left **Here rich violet is used to define the alcove above the bed, while the rest of the wall is papered in a fawn and purple floral design**

bold and rich violets

Stronger shades of mauve and purple have an opulent quality that makes them a good choice for adding a sense of luxury, whether you use them as statement colours on feature walls or go for the subtle approach by blending them with smoky greys and matt blacks to create intimate and sophisticated living spaces.

regal purple The boldest shades of violet have an aura of unabashed decadence that conjures up lush hothouse orchids, ermine and indulgence. This is the colour chosen as a foil for jewels and a wrapping for chocolates so no wonder it has feel-good connotations. Used in moderation (in checked or striped patterns) it can be paired with yellows, golds and deep greens to create a traditional dining room. For a more contemporary effect, try pairing it with paler hues of pink and violet and then adding in plenty of white on woodwork and flooring. Accent colours can include silver and jade green.

grape shades Richer and redder tones are easier on the eye and because they have added warmth they are a good choice for feature

Above **This light-filled contemporary dining area features a swathe of boldest purple on two walls, with a soft grey-pink used to highlight the remaining wall area**

Far left **Red and purple make good bedfellows provided you match the colours carefully. Here a feature wall in a rich grape shade is partnered with a deep wine red, with accents in turquoise, bolder red and orchid pink**

Left **This modern living space uses a rich reddish aubergine in combination with a softer fawn coloured rug and white ceiling and woodwork**

walls in bedrooms. Combine them with harmonious reds (go for rich deep shades rather than strident orange reds if you want this to be a relaxing setting) and you will add a feeling of balance. White can be too harsh a contrast, so choose ivory or cream for walls and woodwork.

aubergine Sophisticated violets with a red-brown tinge add depth and warmth to living spaces. Used over four walls they can become oppressive so consider using them on just one or two walls in combination with paler creams or fawns. These are shades that lack the feminine overtones of paler violets so they are a good choice for contemporary settings, particularly if you combine them with modern sculptural furniture and rough weave textures such as felt, wool and linen.

deep purple Dark almost inky shades of purple are an alternative to black and grey – indeed the three colours can be combined to create a sophisticated variation on black and white schemes. At this intensity purple absorbs almost as much light as black or navy, so only use it in areas where you want to create an intimate 'after dark' setting and add in areas of bright contrasting white on ceiling and woodwork to stop the room from feeling too murky.

Above **Deep purple is layered with black furniture and flooring to create an intimate setting in one corner of a living room. Adding in chrome and glass details and a floor-to-ceiling mirror on one wall increases light levels and adds to the atmosphere**

choose dramatic details

You can really go to town on details with a violet room. Here are easy ways to add drama to your colour scheme.

- In bedrooms dress the bed with a range of opulent materials – plush textures such as velvet and fun fur work well. You can even add a wallhanging to the area behind the bed or hang a canopy above to create a decadent four-poster feel.
- Look for details such as embroidery and crewel work and add your own beaded,

fringed or fur trims to jazz up plain cushions or bedcovers.
- Mix colours as well as textures, combining rich inky mauves with paler pinks and creams. Fawns and soft beiges also help to create a layered effect, softening strong violets.
- With deeper tones of violet introduce flashes of bolder colour – try accents of bright orange, pink or bright yellow. Deep browns and blacks can also be included, but look for reflective textures such as silk and metallic trims.

add stencilled floral motifs

This handpainted flower design is a quick way to transform a plain painted room and it looks particularly effective against a bold backdrop such as violet. Here a naïve flower has been used – which looks most effective when you go for random rather then regular effects. If you are a confident artist you can paint this design freehand. Alternatively, follow the method below.

YOU WILL NEED:

- **Strong card or mylar**
- **Soft pencil**
- **Sharp scissors or craft blade**
- **Low-tack masking tape or adhesive spray**
- **Silver acrylic paint (e.g. stencil paint)**
- **Thin stencil brush**

① First create your stencil flowerhead by drawing a design onto a large sheet of strong card or mylar (available from art shops). You may be confident about doing this freehand, but if not, enlarge the design opposite on a photocopier and then trace it onto the card or mylar using a soft pencil (fig 1).

② Leaving a generous square border around the shape, cut away the inside of the design. Use sharp scissors or a craft knife to do this. Discard the cut out centre and your stencil is ready for use (fig 2). If necessary, create stencils for the flower centre and flower leaf in the same way.

③ Decide on the positioning of your flower – place the flowerhead first – and fix the stencil in place using the masking tape or adhesive spray.

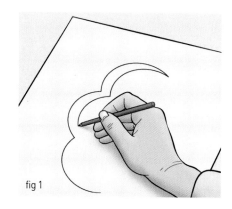

fig 1

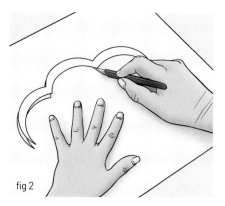

fig 2

④ Stencil round the flowerhead using the stencil paint. Now paint on the flower centre freehand or with a stencil (it will help if you use a ruler to measure from the petals to the centre).

⑤ With your flowerhead in place, use the stencil brush to draw on your flower stalk. Work downwards in a single stroke (you can always touch this up later) and ensure your brush is not overloaded so the paint does not run. Once the stalk is in place finish by painting on the leaf. When the paint is dry remove your stencils and move on to the next flower.

 PRACTICAL TIP

USING STENCIL PAINT Stencilling works best if you apply paint lightly so keep your brush quite dry – have a kitchen towel handy so you can wipe excess paint from the brush before stencilling each section. Remember that you can always paint over your design if you decide you are not happy with it.

Right **Large-scale flowers painted in a silvery grey are a great way to give the handpainted look to plain walls in a dining room**

blue

BLUE IS VERSATILE, OFFERING A SHADE TO SUIT EVERY ROOM. IT ALSO HAS THE ABILITY TO SET THE SCENE WHETHER YOU WANT A NAUTICAL BATHROOM OR A CLASSIC COUNTRY KITCHEN

Blue comes in a multitude of shades, from icy sky tones to jewel colours that conjure up the warmth of the Mediterranean. Pale and mid shades are perfect partners for pinks and whites, while richer hues bring out the best in golden yellows and tropical oranges. This is a segment of the colour wheel that offers a wealth of choice – whatever your room's aspect – and you will find it is one of the easiest of all colours to use as the basis of a successful decorating scheme. This chapter gives advice on picking the perfect shade to match your room's aspect, shows you colours guaranteed to bring blue to life and includes a selection of decorative paint effects to transform walls, fabric and floors.

Right **Pale blue with a hint of duck egg is an easygoing shade that conjures up American country style. It makes a natural partner for deeper blues, rich creams and bolder tones of pink and red**

why choose blue?

Blue offers a shade to suit almost any location and is the basis for some of our favourite decorating themes – from nautical bathrooms to the classic blue and white check found in country schemes. Blue does have a reputation as a cold colour, and it is true that some paler hues have a touch of frost that makes them unsuited to north facing rooms, but choose a shade with green in it and you get duck egg or bold aqua guaranteed to warm up the coldest spot. Blue is also a good mixer – on chintz and floral wallpaper it sits happily alongside pink and yellow, while deeper tones bring reds and dark greens to life. Your toughest decision is which shade to choose as your starting point.

pale blues

Pale blues range from cool grey tones to softer green-blues and sophisticated marine colours. These are among the most adaptable colours for walls, although you may choose to warm them up by mixing them with deeper shades from the same segment of the colour wheel, or introduce contrasts such as pale yellow or apricot to add a more cheerful flavour to the room.

grey-blue
Blues containing hints of grey are naturally restful, making them a good choice for a bedroom or sitting room. If you want to warm up the room, add in details in mauve or warmer shades of blue or accents in buttery yellows. Grey blues are good partners for pale

Below **Simple pale wood furniture adds to the restful atmosphere of this grey-blue bedroom. Canvases above the bed pick out accents of mauve and a jewel blue screen adds a flash of intense colour**

Above **This elegant living room combines a bolder turquoise blue with pale beige carpet and sofa. The strong colour of the walls makes a good foil for the reddish tones of the antique side table**

Left **This pale blue with hints of duck egg makes a good partner for rich buttermilk painted furniture. The deep pile wool rug adds an element of luxury to a plain scheme**

wood and ivory painted furniture, but avoid combining them with dark wood unless the room gets plenty of natural light.

duck egg shades
Blues with hints of green in them have a distinct crossover quality, giving them added warmth that makes them good partners for rich creams, pale pinks and silvery mauves. These are a smart choice for rooms that don't receive much natural light, although pick your colour with care (use tester pots to get the right warm shade) and avoid hues that veer towards peppermint.

towards turquoise
Stronger blues containing hints of green and yellow pigment are good colours for formal living rooms. Containing more warmth, they look particularly good when teamed with mid or dark wood furniture and you can warm them up further by adding in rich beiges, yellows and golds. Stick to clean, white woodwork to keep the effect crisp and fresh and go for neutral wooden floors or carpet. Natural floorings such as sisal and jute also work well against this shade.

blues for bathrooms

Blue is a natural for bathrooms, offering you the chance to mix in cheerful seaside stripes or, if you prefer a more sophisticated spa room feel, elegant stone flooring and silver and chrome details. Here are tips for choosing the right blue, and adding in finishing touches.

- For small rooms with restricted natural light choose a pale aqua blue and add in plenty of white or cream to make the room appear larger. Include reflective elements such as mirrored tiles and chrome accessories and install recessed lighting to make the ceiling seem higher.
- For a simple family bathroom with a nautical flavour paint the walls white, add navy and white wall tiles and introduce accents in cheerful yellow and red stripes – or pink if you prefer a seaside holiday feel. Include beachcomber accessories such as pebbles, shells and natural sponges.
- For Mediterranean bathrooms introduce mosaic-style tiles. These are usually supplied in sheets (usually the size of a large tile) and you can find styles suitable for both walls and floors. Look for greenish blues, or mix tiles in marine blue and softer purple tones.
- In larger bathrooms with a country flavour consider adding tongue-and-groove panelling as an alternative to tiles. This can be painted in a soft duck egg or mid blue and you can continue the effect by adding panelling to the front of the bath. Remember that the panelling will need to be properly sealed with varnish or painted in a kitchen and bathroom paint to make it resistant to moisture.

Left **This sophisticated bathroom combines simple stone flooring with a soft sky blue wall and ceiling. A bolder marine blue is introduced on the wall facing the bath to create a striking focal point**

richer blues

From bold sky colours through lilacs to midnight shades, the darker end of the colour wheel offers a variety of warming blues. These are best combined with paler shades – or you can use them on just one wall and add white to lighten your scheme.

bright sky blue Rich sky shades
have a soft and romantic quality that works well in country-style bedrooms or traditional kitchens. In kitchens you can pair them with buttermilk and pale yellow, while in bedrooms they work well if you add accents in soft grey, muted peach and lilac plus crisp white bedlinen. Keep window treatments simple to maximise natural light.

Below **Bold sky blue creates a romantic backdrop for this light-filled bedroom. The soft eiderdown is in a paler grey-blue shade and tones of lilac and grey are also picked up on the cushion and throw**

lilac tones
Blues containing lilac overtones work well in bedrooms and intimate living rooms, although you need to ensure you choose a tone that is warm if this is a room with restricted natural daylight. Alternatively use it as a colour for a feature wall, mixing it in with white or cream on facing walls. Accessorise with harmonious shades – stronger mauves and blues or paler grey-blues, and introduce soft textures such as silk on cushions and throws.

deep marine shades
Shades that veer towards deep turquoise and marine blue are a bold choice and they need careful handling.

Left **Lilac blues create a soft and feminine setting – perfect for bedrooms or intimate living spaces. Here it is used to create a feature wall around the fireplace, with off-white used on facing walls**

 COLOUR TIP

MIXING BLUES If you want to add depth and warmth to a pale blue decorating scheme, pick out one or two walls in a richer colour. This works best in rooms that receive plenty of natural light and you should paint the area around the window in the paler of the two shades. The darker colour can be used on the facing wall, or use it to highlight a natural focal point such as the area around a fireplace. Try mixing a grey or greenish blue with a richer airforce blue or, if you want a failsafe combination, just pick shades two or three segments apart on the same colour card.

Left **A feature wall in a stronger shade of blue helps to warm up this functional office space. This is a colourscheming technique that works best in rooms that receive plenty of natural light**

You can use them with confidence in rooms with plenty of natural light, but restrict them to a feature wall in a darker setting. Soften the effect by mixing in neutral beiges and fawns or paler blues and greens. Checked and striped fabrics containing harmonious shades of blue, green and pale lilac work particularly well.

midnight blues

Like black, dark blues absorb light so they need the right setting to come into their own. Never use them on all four walls – the effect will be far too oppressive – but you can try a deep blue or navy shade if you have a room that is flooded with sunlight and you want to add a more intimate atmosphere. Combine them with pale blues, turquoises and crisp white or cream. Include plenty of reflective surfaces such as silver and mirrored finishes on furniture and accessories.

Above **This smart marine blue is partnered with crisp white woodwork and a blind in subtle blue-green shades. Plain neutral carpet and elegant rattan and wood furniture add to the simple and contemporary feel**

Left **Midnight blue makes a good choice for defining one wall of this light-filled studio flat. This is a shade that works best in combination with pale and bold blues and you can add in reflective mirrored or silver finishes on furniture and accessories**

design your own artwork

Use tester pots or acrylic paints to design your own customised artworks for displaying above the fireplace or hanging on the wall. This is an easy project and you can match the artwork to your colour scheme or go for bold rainbow effects.

Above **A rainbow of painted squares displayed above the fireplace pick up accents found elsewhere in this cosy sitting room**

YOU WILL NEED:

- **Plain white cardboard mounts or frames**
- **White card cut to fit inside mounts or frames**
- **White acrylic paint**
- **Small paintbrush**
- **Tester pots of emulsion or acrylic paints in your chosen shades**
- **Selection of paintbrushes, sponges or small paint pads**

① Paint the mounts or frames using the white acrylic paint. Leave to dry thoroughly and apply a second coat if necessary.

② Using a brush, sponge or paint pad, paint the cards. Leave to dry and apply a second coat if necessary

③ When the paint is dry, slot the cards inside their mounts ready for displaying on the wall.

Tip: If you prefer sturdier frames, look for unvarnished wood designs (available from craft supply shops). You can go for a clean matt finish for each of your mini canvases or allow the brushstrokes or sponge marks to show. If you use acrylic paint the colours will be more intense.

VARIATIONS

This is also a good way to pick up pattern found elsewhere in your room or introduce luxurious silk or woven textures as art by using offcuts of material. Simply cut squares of fabric to fit inside the mounts and staple or glue them to thin card (use a very thin coat of PVA glue). Leave to dry then slot inside the frames. The fabric may need ironing into place to seal the design.

choose neutral flooring

Blue is such a dominant colour that in all but the largest rooms it is best paired with neutral flooring. Carpet and floorboards in the beige and fawn spectrum work well, adding warmth underfoot and allowing you to add in additional neutral accessories. Grey can also work, but steelier tones are best reserved for working rooms such as kitchens as they have an industrial edge that can make the room feel too functional. White or cream-painted floorboards are natural partners for pale and turquoise blues, particularly if you are creating a country-style setting. If you want to add additional colours go for rugs in stripes or florals that either include blue or pick up accent colours found elsewhere in your scheme.

Right **This soft fawn carpet adds warmth to a cosy blue and cream papered bedroom. The cream bedroom furniture adds a traditional edge, while deeper tones of grey blue are introduced in the eiderdown and cotton bedlinen**

 QUICK IDEA TIP

MOOD-SETTING STAMPED WALLS

A stamped design is a good way to break up a dark blue wall – particularly if you choose a contrasting neutral colour. Here we chose a 1960s-style white motif. This pattern appears random but in fact the motifs are placed in lines. If you are not confident applying the motifs by eye, use a plumb line and vertical rule and mark on pencil or chalk points at regular intervals before you start (stick on a sliver of masking tape if you prefer not to mark the wall. Work from the top down using a firm pressing action and remember to use stamping ink to avoid colour runs. Stop at regular intervals and stand back from the wall to check you have placed the pattern correctly. Remember you can always paint over motifs and start again if you are not happy with the result. If you want a simpler and quicker method, restrict your stamp pattern to part of the wall – a large square or rectangle placed centrally would achieve a similar dreamy effect. If you choose this option make sure your stamped panel matches the scale of the room and position it at just above eye height for maximum impact.

Left **Space-age walls are easy to create if you use deep blue and add a circular stamped motif in white**

add red accents for drama

Above **Deep wine red is used for a feature wall in an apartment kitchen, adding a focal point that bridges the divide between functional working area and the more 'social' and intimate end of the room**

Variations on red – from traffic light colours to burgundy – add warmth to blues making them classic pairings to bring a scheme to life. If you are using red and blue paint on walls or furniture pick both shades at the same time and test them on your walls because if you get it wrong the effect can be harsh or overwhelming.

- Don't combine shades of equal intensity if you are combining blue and red on walls. It is far more effective to go for one pale shade and one bold or rich shade – for instance a pale blue with a rich burgundy. You can then pick up the bolder red in accessories or add in a third deeper shade of blue as accent colour.

- Cheerful pillar-box reds are a classic in children's rooms. They can be too strong for walls but look effective if you introduce them on bedlinen and rugs. Check out office supply shops for well-priced functional furniture such as bright red metal filing cupboards, plastic or steel-topped desks and office chairs.

- If you prefer to tone things down a little deep rose pinks are also a good foil for blues, but choose your shade with care. Opt for pinks with red in them (rather than cooler lilac) and go for a warm turquoise or aqua blue. This stops your room from feeling cold, but looks most effective if you pick one colour for walls and restrict the other to accents and accessories.

Right **A variation on the blue and red theme, this stylish living room pairs duck egg blue with neutral soft furnishings and accents in orangey brown**

Left **Red and blue office style furniture adds a dash of warmth to a teenager's bedroom. Stripes in a richer shade are placed midway down, breaking up the expanse of blue wall**

A VARIATION ON THE CLASSIC BLUE AND RED PAIRING, THIS ELEGANT COUNTRY-STYLE LIVING ROOM COMBINES RICH DUCK EGG BLUE WALLS WITH A PALER TONING SHADE ON CEILING AND SOFA AND A RICH ORANGEY BROWN ON FURNITURE AND ACCENTS

create stencilled effects

Stencils are an inexpensive way to create bespoke effects on walls, floors and fabric. You can buy a huge range of designs – from traditional floral motifs to large-scale animal and abstract designs. Before you start you need to decide on your motif and how you intend to use it on your wall. You can either go for an all over pattern such as the motif pictured right, or design 'wall art' effects with large-scale stencils placed randomly. Repeat patterns require more careful measuring and it is worth the time spent marking out their positioning as you are less likely to end up with out-of-line images.

fig 1

fig 2

fig 3

YOU WILL NEED:

- **Large ruler and pencil, plumb line and spirit level**
- **Readymade mylar stencils**
- **Low-tack masking tape or adhesive spray**
- **Stencil paint**
- **Stencil brushes**
- **Kitchen roll**
- **Small artist's brush**

① If you are going for an all-over pattern use a ruler and pencil to mark out the position of each stencil using a plumb line for vertical positioning and a spirit level for horizontal positioning. Work from the top of the wall downwards. For random 'wall art' effects, work out your positioning by deciding on the best focal points – ideally you want your images to start at just above eye height (fig 1).

② Fix your stencil in place using low-tack masking tape or spray. Make sure you fix it at all four corners (fig 2).

③ Load your brush with stencil paint and then wipe off excess – the brush should be almost dry to the touch. Using a firm dabbing action, apply the stencil paint ensuring you cover all areas. Work along stencil cut lines rather than dabbing into them (this minimises paint runs underneath the stencil). Leave to dry. If you are creating a two-tone design, leave one colour to dry before painting the other one.

④ Remove the stencil and move onto the next area. Once the whole wall has been completed you can use a small artist's brush to touch up areas, or introduce darker shading to parts of the motif (fig 3).

Tips

- If you have glossy walls you may have to sand them first.
- Practise first on a piece of card so you know how much paint to use.
- Save time by buying several stencils if you are going for an all over pattern.

🖐 **DECORATOR'S NOTE**

BUYING STENCILS You pay more for mylar but the stencils are far more durable than cardboard and can be folded over for tricky areas such as corners and where wall meets skirting board. For wall art effects choose a large design and remember that grouping two or three bold motifs together creates a far more effective focal point than placing them at regular intervals around the wall.

Above **Large-scale motifs transform a plain wall into a romantic country-style setting. It is important to vary the motif if you want to create this pictorial toile de jouy effect**

ADD PATTERN TO FABRIC

Cotton and silk fabrics take stencilled designs well – so this is a good way to co-ordinate walls and soft furnishings as you can continue a design onto curtains, bedlinen or cushion cover. Make sure you use specialist fabric paint. This is a water-based solution that you allow to dry and then fix using a hot iron. The fabric is then washable. Lay the fabric flat before you start stencilling – it may help to pin or peg it so that it lies absolutely straight.

Above **A delicate dragonfly and leaf design is used to dress up plain white curtains. The motif was painted using specialist paint and sealed with a hot iron**

STENCILLING A FLOOR

Stencilling a floor can be easier than tackling a wall, not least because the paint is less likely to run and your arms do not get so tired. Go for large-scale designs if you can – mosaic effects work particularly well. Use a multi-surface paint and remember that your design will need to be sealed afterwards with a clear matt acrylic varnish. A simple border design looks more effective than an all over stencil pattern if you are stencilling onto painted wooden floorboards.

Right **Plain floor tiles get a Moroccan-style mosaic pattern using shades of blue, pink and brown. The pattern looks complex but it was created in layers using three different sized stencils**

green

NATURE'S MOST HARMONIOUS SHADE, GREEN WORKS EQUALLY WELL INSIDE OUR HOMES AND IT MIXES EFFORTLESSLY WITH THE REST OF THE COLOUR SPECTRUM

Green is all around us in nature – from cool aqua hues to the rich colours of woodland foliage. Pale fern or mint greens are great mixers that are guaranteed to create a soft and easygoing setting when paired with natural woods or combined with reds and pinks in fresh florals and checks. Add in a touch more cool blue and you get muted greens that work effectively as a backdrop for sophisticated living rooms and tranquil hallways. Rich tartan greens are the most atmospheric shades of all, conjuring up Christmas cheer, grand country houses and fireside comfort.

Right **Soft fern greens create a tranquil living room, with co-ordinating textured paper used to define adjoining walls. This is a look that works best with neutral pale wood floors and furniture**

why choose green?

Green is all around us, so perhaps that is why it is easy to take it for granted and forget its unique properties. No other colour can be used to define a decorating theme so quickly – if you want Eastern opulence look to jade green; for tropical intensity choose lime. More useful in our homes are the multitude of subtle shades that add tranquillity and pair up beautifully with blues (despite the old saying), reds and neutrals. Perhaps green's chief virtue is that even the boldest tones are invariably easy to live with, making them a natural basis for almost any decorating style and adaptable enough to add colour without dominating a room.

Left This muted blue-green is used to define the walls on either side of the chimney-breast, reinforcing the Eastern theme of a living room furnished with Chinoiserie furniture and accessories

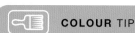 **COLOUR** TIP

OPT FOR STRONGER GREENS While subtle pale and neutral shades work with most other colours, it is usually best to be a little bolder when you are working with green paint. At their palest greens have a washed out and utilitarian quality that reacts badly with natural light, so pick two or three shades down from the top of the colour card to ensure you get a definite colour. You can always restrict the green to one or two feature walls or use it to define the area under a dado rail. And if you prefer neutral shades for the walls pick a cream or off-white instead (go for yellow or orange-toned neutrals for warmth) and then add in strong greens via accents.

pale and mid greens

Paler greens are not always muted – crisp mint greens provide a boost for hallways or kitchens, while acid shades add a tropical flavour to bedrooms and living areas. Tone it down a little though and you can add a 'back to nature' quality that works well in any setting.

crisp mint Minty colours are fresh and cheerful, making them useful if you want to lift a dull hallway or add light to a family rooms. Look to shades with the right balance of blue and yellow – too blue and your room will appear cold and unwelcoming. These fresh shades make good partners for yellow and pale peachy orange or try them in combination with bright white walls and glossy white woodwork.

soft aqua Pale aqua conjures up water, making it a popular alternative to blue in bathrooms. It works well in combination with white, but you can also add in accents in harmonious shades of blue and yellow. This is also a shade to consider for kitchens if you want to design a slick contemporary scheme that does not feel too harsh and industrial, since aqua works well with steel and pale wood.

Below **Mint is a great choice for high-traffic areas such as hallways. Here a crisp green is used for the area under a dado rail, with soft peachy-orange used for the area above it**

leaf and khaki greens Leaf and khaki greens are adaptable shades that suit contemporary living areas and bedrooms. They are also good colours for studies and home offices, particularly in combination with pale wood furniture, white woodwork and natural elements such as plants, stone flooring and bamboo matting. Add accents in silver, or combine them with pale grey for a more masculine setting. Choose your lighting with care, going for layered effects by placing lamps at different heights. Use halogen rather than tungsten bulbs to ensure you get a flattering blue rather than unflattering yellowish light.

Right **Aqua is a natural alternative to blue in bathrooms – imparting a sense of warmth and tranquillity. Here mosaic-effect tiles are used for the wall and bath panel, with larger tiles defining the area around the bath**

Left **Adding a deeper shade at half room height adds interest to a garden room. Use toning greens and ensure the paler shade is used for the top half of the room or it will look unbalanced**

add silver circles

This project is easy to do and you can vary the size of the circles to suit your room's dimensions. The silver finish works particularly well if you combine it with a feature wall in a contemporary shade such as fresh mint or aqua green.

YOU WILL NEED:

- **Spirit level**
- **Long ruler**
- **Pencil**
- **Compass (optional)**
- **Strong card**
- **Low-tack masking tape or adhesive spray**
- **Silver stencil or acrylic paint**
- **Small stencil brush**

① Use the spirit level to mark a horizontal guideline midway down your wall. This will be the point where the centre of each circle sits. Mark two additional guidelines 7.5 cm (3 in) above and below the first guide line to help you ensure accurate positioning of the circles (fig 1).

② Decide on the size of circles you want and then create stencilled circular outlines using strong card. You can use cups and plates as surfaces to draw round, or guarantee accuracy with a compass. Cut these out carefully using a craft knife (rest the card on a pile of newspapers to protect the surface underneath).

Above **Silver circles are used to create a simple paint effect in this cream and mint green living room. Shades of silver and grey are also picked out in the deep-pile rug and cushions**

③ Using the horizontal guide lines to help you, fix stencils to the walls before you start so you can check you are happy with their positioning. It may also help if you use the ruler to get them equal distance apart (fig 2).

④ Carefully infill each stencil with the silver stencil paint, making sure you do not overload your brush. Leave to dry and then remove the stencils.

Tips

- Decorate the wall with same size circles for a quicker paint effect.
- Use this basic method to create a multitude of simple stencils e.g. flowers and stars.
- Use self-adhesive foil shapes for a simple alternative to stencilling (see page 70).

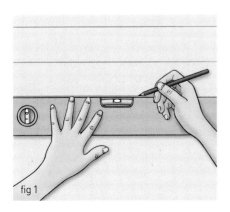

fig 1

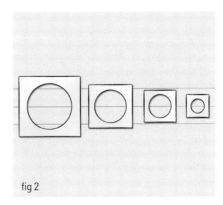

fig 2

three-tone stripes

This simple colour gradation effect is easy to do and relies for its impact on using tonal greens. Pick your shades from the same colour card to guarantee good results and remember to allow plenty of drying time between coats.

YOU WILL NEED:

- **Plumb line**
- **Long ruler**
- **Pencil**
- **Masking tape**
- **Vinyl matt emulsion or acrylic paint in three toning shades**
- **Paint pads**
- **Brushes**

① Paint the entire wall area to be decorated in the palest shade of green. Leave to dry.

② Using a ruler measure the depth of the wall and decide where the colour bands should go – you can place them equally, or vary the depth so that one colour covers a larger wall area. Use a plumb line and ruler to mark on the point where the second and third colours begin.

③ Place masking tape above the first rule and below the second so your middle stripe is the right width.

④ Now paint on the middle stripe using a paint pad to ensure even coverage. Start by creating a clean edge at top and bottom and then infill the stripe using a larger paint pad if necessary. Leave to dry. Remove the masking tape and you will have a two-tone wall, with a band of deeper colour in the middle.

⑤ For the final and deepest coloured stripe re-measure the wall, add a pencil rule where the final stripe should begin then place masking tape above this rule. Paint using a paint pad as before, leave to dry and then remove masking tape.

Above **Adding stripes in toning shades is a good way to pick out a small wall area. Here pale to deep greens are used to add interest to the area above a low storage and display unit**

Tip: This may seem a time-consuming way of producing stripes but it is far easier to get a clean and accurate finish if you work down the wall, applying darker stripes over the top of paler colours. If you are confident with a paint pad you may be able to paint in the final stripe by eye – the trick is to work quickly and in one smooth motion without recharging the pad with paint. Remember you can always touch up wobbly edges later with a small paintbrush or pad.

pattern mixing with green

Green comes alive when it is used in combination with other colours. More contemporary patterns may pair it with silvers and greys, but there are tried and trusted colourways that are well suited to more traditional decorating schemes.

garden greens
Paler shades of green are most at home in chintz and floral designs, particularly in combination with other garden colours such as rose pink and buttercup yellow. These are soft and appealing combinations for wallpaper or curtains and work well if you add in checks and stripes on accessories.

lime greens
More acid shades also work well as part of a co-ordinated scheme – think tropical and pair them with bright pinks, bold oranges and turquoise-blue tones. You can also mix them with softer blue greens for a muted effect. Try them in children's rooms as part of a co-ordinated scheme, or introduce a swathe of lime on a feature wall in a family room or study.

mossy colours
Richer shades of moss green are a classic background shade for tartan checks and they work beautifully with shades of violet and pink (think heather colours) or, if you want a richer effect try them with deep blues and reds. These are partnerships that generally look overwhelming over a large wall area, but you can use them with confidence on curtains, throws and cushions to add depth and comfort to a room scheme. Try introducing them to a room where the walls are painted in a muted olive green.

Above **This pretty floral wallpaper mixes two shades of garden green with a contrasting pink. Garden greens work equally well with buttercup yellows, soft apricot and rich creams**

Right **This fun children's room features a soft lime spotted wallpaper and blue and lime patterned curtains and bedlinen. The same bold green is used to decorate the bedside furniture**

crossover colours

Greens that contain a lot of blue take on a sophisticated edge that can be particularly effective in period decorating schemes, although the boldest turquoise shades are a good way to create a contemporary setting.

duck egg tones
No two duck egg blues are ever quite the same – rather like the eggs they are named after – but they range from distinctly blue tones through to almost greens. They are invariably pale shades that add subtle elegance to the walls of a light-filled bedroom or living room. Alternatively use them to give a colourful twist to woodwork. They look effective

Right **A vibrant turquoise green wall is combined with a more muted sage green chair. The cushion picks out the softer green tones as well as bolder reds and blues**

Below **Duck egg tones add sophistication to period schemes. Here a blueish tone is used to decorate half-height panelling in a living room, with a paler grey toned neutral above**

framing a large sash window (ensure walls are painted a paler toning shade or a creamy neutral) or used to cover tongue-and-groove panelling in a bathroom, hallway or kitchen.

turquoise
This vibrant tropical colour is a good choice for contemporary decorating. Try mixing it with pinks or reds if you want to turn up the heat or add bright whites for a crisper effect. It can be too bold over a large area, but like lime green it makes an effective choice for a feature wall. It works best in areas that receive a lot of natural light so remember to keep window treatments simple and neutral to maximize the sunshine effect.

jade greens
The deepest green-blue tones were popular in Art Deco decorating and their aura of film star glamour makes them a good choice for accents and accessories in a boudoir style bedroom. Over a larger area they are best in combination with other colours – silver or pewter tones are classic partnerships although they also look effective against gold and bronze. Mix jade and black accents against a pale neutral wall for a striking focal point.

stronger greens

More powerful greens are good colours if you want to create a focal point, reinforce an intimate atmosphere or add timeless sophistication in a living area. Here are three schemes where they are used to dramatic effect.

strong peppermint

Very bold mint shades have a stimulating effect that makes them a great choice for feature walls in working rooms such as kitchens and studies. On its own this is a colour that can be too harsh but add in mellow wood tones with a yellowish hue and reflective elements such as silver and chrome (perfect for a contemporary kitchen) and you get a winning combination. Make sure the wall is prepared properly if you are painting in such a strong colour as it will show every crack and flaw. For more intense tones try using an acrylic paint rather than vinyl matt emulsion.

Above **Rich tartan check carpet and traditional leather chairs create a clubroom feel in this cosy living room. The fireplace is painted in the same sage green as the walls**

Left **A feature wall in a bold minty shade adds atmosphere to this contemporary neutral kitchen. It is an effective foil to yellowish woods such as beech and pine**

sage Mellow tones of sage green create a naturally intimate atmosphere redolent of gentlemen's clubs and old country houses. This is a warm-up colour, designed to add intimacy and a relaxing atmosphere to rooms where the main purpose is to curl up around a cosy fire. Restrict it to rooms that get plenty of natural light, or settings that are used mainly in the evenings. Add in dark leather furniture, mellow wood plus tartan check furnishings or accessories.

dark olive Olive greens have a sophisticated edge that works equally well with traditional or contemporary furniture. Only choose darker shades if you have a large and light-filled room and mix in plenty of white on woodwork and ceilings. Floors should be neutral wood or carpet, or opt for pale painted boards.

Right **This elegant reception room combines deep olive green with dark leather furniture and bright white woodwork. Accents are restricted to an oversized mirror over the fireplace and a few simple vases**

add warmth with traditional flooring

Greens generally work best with neutral wood or carpet, but sometimes this combination leaves a room feeling cold or unwelcoming. Try more traditional elements if you want to add warmth and period credentials to your scheme.

add natural stone Introducing a strong coloured flooring helps to warm up pale coloured walls and this can be particularly useful in large or high-ceilinged rooms, or in areas such as kitchens that already contain a lot of natural wood. Choose a complementary colour such as deep slate grey or look for a flooring that contains a muted green within the pattern.

Left **A deep grey slate introduces the comfort factor in this rustic pine kitchen. Greenish hues within the slate help to warm up the duck egg blue walls**

introduce contrasting carpet

In Victorian and Edwardian homes muted olive and sage greens were often combined with russet browns and oranges and this nature-inspired combination looks particularly effective in areas such as hallways where restricted natural daylight means you need to add warmth to your scheme. If you go for a contrasting carpet include pattern in curtains or upholstered chairs that picks up the colours of both wall and floor. If walls are plain it adds interest to your scheme if you choose a patterned design on the flooring – especially if you are covering a large area. If this is a narrow room, choose a simple floral or graphic design or introduce a plain carpet with a patterned border (for more tips on using carpet to add decorative effects see page 36).

Right An Arts and Crafts-style floral design on the curtain helps to link the colours of walls and carpet in this traditional hallway. The introduction of white on skirtings and hall table adds freshness to the scheme

 DECORATING TIP

INTRODUCE INTEREST WITH TEXTURE Texture is a great way to add depth to a green scheme, particularly if you add in accents and accessories that introduce a feeling of light.

- Pale and mid greens take on a fresher hue if they include white or cream on accents, so introduce checks and stripes on cushions and curtains or add in woven materials with a muted floral or geometric design. It is important to keep a sense of freshness in pale schemes so avoid heavy plush or raised materials, opting instead for woven cottons and natural linens or lightweight silks. Add in reflective silver or opalescent details with a few well chosen ornaments.

- Rich greens are good partners for luxurious textures such as velvet and heavy silk. A variety of rich colours help to reinforce the scheme's natural credentials – look for autumnal browns and oranges on cushions and curtains and add in accents such as gilt, copper and bronze on picture frames, bowls and candlesticks.

Right Rich jade is the perfect foil for copper and bronze as well as autumnal oranges and browns. Here silk cushions are used to pick out the sumptuous green and brown floral wallpaper

stencil nature motifs on tiles

This green bathroom was decorated with stencilled motifs inspired by nature. This is an easy way to customise plain white tiles but they need to be baked in the oven to seal the design so paint on your motif before you attach them to the wall.

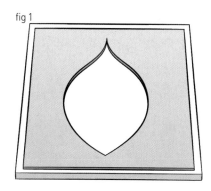
fig 1

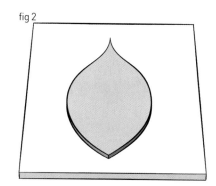
fig 2

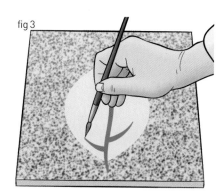
fig 3

YOU WILL NEED:

- **Ceramic wall tiles**
- **Leaf shape cut from cardboard (retain both leaf shape and outline)**
- **Spray adhesive**
- **Ceramic paint in a variety of greens**
- **Ceramic outliner in brown or gold**
- **Stencil brushes**

🖐 **DECORATOR'S** NOTE

Left You can add in additional natural details by painting plain wooden squares with flowers

① For the green leaf design attach the outline leaf stencil to the tile using spray mount (this will fill in the colour of the leaf). You can either paint this to create a matt finish or, as shown here, dab paint on using the ends of a very dry stencil brush to create a soft stippled effect. Leave the tile to dry (fig 1).

② For the white leaf design attach the leaf shape stencil using spray adhesive (this means the leaf will remain white).

FLOWER PICTURES You can add additional stencilled details to dress up your bathroom. Here a pretty cowslip motif was used to create a set of three pictures. The designs were stencilled onto plain wood squares previously painted to match the window frames. Each flower design is slightly different but the stalks line up on all three frames to create a unified effect.

Use the same stippling technique to paint the tile and leave to dry (fig 2).

③ Once all the tiles are dry infill the leaf veins using ceramic outliner (fig 3).

④ When you are happy with the design of the tiles (at this stage they are still washable), bake them according to the manufacturer's instructions.

Notes
- You can buy ready-made stencils to produce a 'reverse' effect – they are known as layered stencils.
- Ceramic paint will seal tiles to make them washable – ideal for bathrooms. Usually the tiles are baked for around 35 minutes in a hot oven.

Tip: If you want to add more 'splodgy' effects to the background of the tiles try flicking paint onto the tiles from the end of a stiff brush (a toothbrush is ideal) so that it lands in small droplets – a technique known as spattering.

Right **This two-tone leaf motif was created using a layered stencil**

yellow

ADD INSTANT SUNSHINE BY CHOOSING A BOLD YELLOW SHADE OR COMBINE SUBTLER BUTTERY TONES WITH STRONGER HUES TO CREATE THE MOST RELAXED OF DECORATING SCHEMES

Yellow is the classic warm-up colour and we often use it in a more dilute form in a whole range of neutrals – from off-whites to buttery clotted creams. Pale yellows are country classics, useful in check and floral patterns or as wall colours in a north facing room. Warmer shades capture a more Mediterranean flavour, making them a favourite shade for both rustic and contemporary kitchens. Add a hint of acid green or orange and you get a perfect colour for feature walls and bold accents. There are endless variations to choose from, but some yellows can be far more strident than they appear on the colour card so we include foolproof colours for every setting as well as advice on colour and pattern mixing to create schemes that work.

Right **Bold yellow walls add warmth to this kitchen-diner. The effect is tempered by painting units in a paler creamy yellow while floor and worktop are in a natural wood finish**

why choose yellow?

It is hard to fault yellow as a background colour, with its tried-and-trusted abilities to warm up cold rooms and offset the gloom of grey northern skies. Although it is such a useful (and well used) colour in our homes subtle variations of tone and shade make all the difference to the quality of light and the environment you create. Go for strong yellows and you have a bold and stimulating setting that suits kitchens, offices and hallways. But choose a buttery or caramel yellow and you create a relaxing ambience that suits living rooms and bedrooms.

Left **Strong caramel accents are used to pick out the bath and blind in this elegant yellow bathroom, with a paler tonal shade used for the panelled walls**

pale yellows

Ranging from clotted creams through to stronger tones with hints of caramel brown, pale shades are the perfect backdrop to rooms where you want to add a sense of light and warmth.

rich cream This is a shade that can act as a neutral, but with its hints of yellow pigment it makes a perfect backdrop to country-style schemes. Pair it with cream or off white-painted furniture for a muted and layered effect, or add in stronger tones of yellow and contrasts such as blue to intensify the colour of your walls. Keep woodwork and ceilings white to heighten the contrast.

vanilla This is a soft and muted shade that suits bedrooms and kitchens and can be combined with florals and cheerful checks and stripes to add warmth without making too strong a colour statement. It can appear too bland in sunny rooms unless you introduce stronger

Right **With its neutral properties, the palest yellow works well with off-whites and creams. Here it is used to create a classic country style dining room**

Below **Vanilla yellow makes a good choice for kitchens, particularly if you accessorise with blues and browns. Here it has been paired with natural wood-effect worktops and flooring**

elements, so try mixing it with pinks and greens or even stronger contrast tones such as navy or reddish brown.

primrose This is the classic pale to mid yellow, with just enough depth to make it a good foil for warmer shades such as red and blue. You can use it with confidence in just about any setting and it adds a cheerful quality to social areas such as living rooms and kitchens. It is a practical choice because you can accessorise it with contemporary or traditional details (and change colours around when you want to update your scheme). It also works well with more neutral elements such as wood and stone floors.

caramel yellow With its hints of brown/orange, this is a much richer and more sophisticated shade, capable of holding its own when mixed with accents of fawn and terracotta. The right textures add to its air of sophistication so look for linens and raw silk fabrics and choose a matt finish for walls.

Left **Primrose yellow is an easygoing choice for kitchens and living areas. Here it is used to add warmth to a high-ceilinged conservatory dining area**

COLOUR TIP

Above **Grey panelling is paired with a bold yellow in this light-filled breakfast room – creating an aura of calm and adding a sophisticated twist to a sunny scheme**

TRY MIXING IT WITH GREY Grey is an unusual contrast to yellow, but this is a combination that can add sophistication to everyday rooms, particularly if you use it on woodwork or accessories (stripes and checks work well). It also has the ability to tone down yellow's sunshine properties – useful if you want to add an aura of calm to a yellow room that is flooded with sunshine. Choose your grey with care: in functional areas such as kitchens it is best to choose a mid-tone without any hints of violet, while in bedrooms you can go for softer dove grey if you want to create a more feminine ambience. It works well in combination with mid-coloured woods or you can introduce more contemporary elements such as chrome and steel.

pattern mixing with yellow

With its nearly neutral qualities, paler yellow can be combined with blue, red, violet or green – making it an excellent choice in checked, striped or floral patterns or as a background wall colour. Stronger tones can be harder to mix – you need to match intensities and be prepared for showstopping effects. Here are two daring colour scheming techniques that work.

rainbow effect
In family rooms and children's bedrooms yellow can be used as the basis of a rainbow colourscheme, where lots of cheerful colours are introduced via patterns and accessories. Bold shades of orange and red are natural partners, but you can also try almost contrasts such as turquoise and bold blue. The best way to achieve the effect is to keep walls and floor plain and introduce pattern on curtains, rugs and accessories such as cushions and throws.

Right Yellow can be used as the backdrop for rainbow schemes – a great choice for playrooms. Tone things down by adding white and neutral elements on flooring and woodwork

citrus combinations
For really bold effects mix yellow with other citrus shades. Combined with orange it takes on a stronger Mediterranean hue that works brilliantly in kitchens or family rooms. But if you also add turquoise and bright pink it moves further south, conjuring up sun-drenched Caribbean style. For an edgier and more daring combination try it with strong green. The effect is particularly intense if you introduce shades of rich lime – you will find the yellow takes on a zingy green edge. This is a look to be handled judiciously so restrict it to larger rooms that receive plenty of natural light. If you want to cool things down a little also include softer pale greens (mossy shades work well) plus plenty of white or cream on furniture and woodwork.

Left For an acid flavour mix strong yellow with deep lime green. Here a waterlily pattern is set against bold yellow walls, with softer green accents to temper the colour-drenched effect

add multicoloured stripes

This stripe is created by painting a white panel onto a bold yellow wall and then infilling with colours that co-ordinate with the rug and seats. It is a dramatic effect that is actually very easy to create.

Left **A band of stripes across the width of one wall adds a rainbow effect to this orange and yellow room. The stripes are painted to pick out the colours found in the rug and children's chairs**

YOU WILL NEED:

- **Spirit level**
- **Ruler**
- **Pencil**
- **Masking tape**
- **Acrylic paint or vinyl matt emulsion in a variety of bold colours**
- **Paint pads**

① First decide on the position of your band. Use the spirit level to ensure a straight edge and mask off the area, placing the tape carefully. You may find it easier to do this in sections if the band is across an expanse of wall, but ensure the tape overlaps so the paint does not leak beyond the edge you have created.

② Using acrylic or vinyl matt emulsion paint apply the white as your base. Leave to dry as per manufacturer's instructions and then apply a second coat. Leave the masking tape along the bottom of the band in place.

③ Once the paint is dry decide on the design you wish to create within the white band. Here the stripes are different widths, but you could choose square or geometric shapes. Mask off the top of the first section to be painted (you will need to work from the bottom up) and infill with paint. Leave each section to dry thoroughly before applying new masking tape and painting the adjoining colour – it will speed things up considerably if you leave a band of white between each coloured stripe.

 DECORATOR'S NOTE

CREATING STRIPES For the thinner stripes use a smaller paint pad or a radiator roller if you prefer. Use acrylic paint to create a more intense colour. You can seal your design with clear acrylic varnish if you want to protect it.

rich yellows

Stronger yellows make more of a statement so you need to plan your room scheme with care, balancing the intensity of your walls by introducing accents that can hold their own.

warm fawn-yellow
This is a sophisticated muted yellow, useful for contemporary living areas where you want to include darker wood and rich neutrals such as caramel and taupe. You can use accents of soft red and add stronger accents of rich reddish brown on furniture and accents. Avoid introducing strong or acid yellows – this should be a restrained setting – and pay attention to textures on soft furnishings, choosing matt or textured woven materials to add tactile qualities to the scheme.

sunshine yellow
Bold sunshine yellows create a stimulating environment that suits contemporary kitchens and working spaces such as home offices. If this is a room you use a lot –

Below Soft fawn-yellow walls make the perfect backdrop to a cosy living space. Mix in rich neutrals such as caramel and taupe and choose tactile textures for soft furnishings

Right **Sunshine yellow makes a good choice in functional spaces such as kitchens and home offices, where it adds a bold and energising atmosphere. Mix in greys and natural woods to soften its strident qualities**

for instance a kitchen diner – you may want to temper its sunny qualities with more sophisticated elements such as steel grey or natural wood. It is a useful colour for adding light to north facing rooms, or for areas where there is no natural daylight at all. Do ensure you get the overhead lighting right. Recessed halogen spotlights will add a softer bluer effect (rather than the yellow of tungsten bulbs) and make it easier to work. Set the lighting on a dimmer switch or layer the effect with wall lights if you also want to use this room for entertaining or relaxing.

orange-yellow This is a mellow yellow, thanks to the hints of orange in its make up, making it is easier to live with than the boldest sunshine and acidic yellows. Consider it as an alternative to these shades if you want a strong colour but a more relaxing atmosphere in a kitchen or living room. It can hold its own against stronger oranges and bright reds but you can also add in marine blues and leaf greens on accents – or try pairing it with deep red and chocolate browns. It is worth considering as a colour for a feature wall as it can add both warmth and the illusion of space to small or low ceilinged areas. It works particularly well against white, but you could also mix in a little pale grey on woodwork or furniture if you want to introduce an element of sophistication.

Left **Orange yellows add a mellow Mediterranean quality to room schemes – perfect in combination with bold reds to create a bistro flavour in the corner of this sunny kitchen**

choose the right accessories

You are spoiled for choice when it comes to picking details that work with a yellow scheme so your best approach is to consider the mood you are trying to create and then select accordingly.

- For elegant pale yellow rooms choose muted colours – soft pinks and reds work well as do textured creams, ivories and beiges. Go for a blended approach, mixing two or three accent colours on cushions, lampshades and ornaments.

- Caramel yellows have a sophisticated flavour that works well with subtle details such as gold and copper trims on cushions and gilt picture frames. Add in smoked glass bowls and crackle-glazed ceramics.

- If you are working with the more strident sunshine yellows keep accents muted – it is best not to try and compete. Grey and metallic details add sophistication and have a neutral quality. If you want a stronger colour accent just choose one shade – for instance a rich blue or green – and use it sparingly.

- Orange yellows are more forgiving and you can add a Mediterranean feel by combining oranges, reds and blues – even touches of violet work. Mix textures and colours but pick up these same colour themes through patterns – introducing stripes and checks on textiles and bold flashes of colour on details such as pictures.

Above **Orange yellows work well with bold primaries such as red and blue. Add in checked and striped patterns to pick up the same colour themes**

 COLOUR TIP

COLOURS FOR LINKING ROOMS Yellow works well with pale orange tones, particularly if you want to link adjoining rooms through colour and still create a subtle demarcation line. It works particularly well as a colour link between practical and relaxation zones – for instance dining rooms that lead off a kitchen or hallway. It is important to keep some common features so stick to the same flooring or link the two rooms by choosing soft furnishings or a rug that share common colour or design themes. Stick to soft tones for best effect, a primrose yellow for the kitchen or hallway and a peach or apricot tone for the dining room is a classic combination that adds warmth without looking too strident.

Left **Soft apricot is used to define a dining area that leads off this yellow hallway. Paler wood flooring helps to link the two adjoining rooms**

create a bold theme with accents

If you want to introduce a yellow focal point to a room without committing to the boldest of shades try using them as accents instead. Paint or paper walls in a soft almost neutral shade and add a strong sunshine or acid yellow through details such as cushions, vases or even a simple graphic image on the wall. The advantage of this colour scheming technique is that you can change your room around simply and inexpensively if you tire of sunshine effects. And since pale yellow is a good backdrop colour you can introduce red, blue or neutral accents further down the line.

Right **Strong yellow creates an arresting focal point in this contemporary living room – but this is actually an almost neutral room with pale walls, furniture and floor, making it easy to change its appearance simply by switching accessories**

⌗ PRACTICAL TIP

LIGHT AND SHADE EFFECTS Yellow is such a warm colour that it can be almost overpowering in a sunny room. A similar dazzling effect can be created after dark if you choose standard overhead light fittings with tungsten bulbs since these cast a naturally yellow light and the effect can be too bright against yellow walls. The solution to both problems is to create light filters. In very bright rooms add voile or muslin panels to screen the sun's rays – look for checked or floral patterns so that the light is filtered unevenly as this produces attractive dappled effects. Alternatively, install Venetian or pinprick-design roller blinds so you can adjust the level of light easily. For night time introduce side lights for adding warmth without glare – cream parchment or fabric shades are better for softening the light than yellow ones. Also consider swapping your overhead light fitting for wall lights so the light is cast up rather than down. In working rooms such as kitchens and offices, install halogen task lighting – illuminating the area above a desk or kitchen worksurface is both practical and atmospheric.

Left **Yellow is a great colour for adding warmth but in sunny rooms it is a good idea to filter and soften the light by introducing voile or muslin panels to windows**

transform kitchen cupboards with paint

Add paint to transform tired kitchen door fronts. You can buy specialist paints that will cover almost all surfaces and you can even paint the doors in situ.

YOU WILL NEED:

- **Screwdriver**
- **Rubber gloves**
- **Sugar soap**
- **Sponge**
- **Small and medium paint brushes**
- **Kitchen cupboard paint (see Tip, below)**

① First prepare your kitchen doors for painting. Remove the door handles. Make up the sugar soap according to manufacturer's instructions (usually it comes as a powder you mix in solution with warm water) and sponge the cupboard doors, paying particular attention to any panelling and cornicing. Do not miss out this first step as paint will not adhere to grease and grime (fig 1).

② Once cupboards are clean and dry start painting your door and drawer fronts – ensure they are open so you get even coverage up to the edges and do one cupboard or drawer at a time. You may want to prop them open before you start painting and mask the surrounding floor and worktop areas with tape.

Above **It is easy to update kitchen cupboards with paint. This kitchen was given the two-tone effect by combining a soft beige with bold orange yellow**

③ Use the smaller brush to tackle small areas such as side panelling and cornicing and work from the top down, going with the grain (fig 2). Use the larger brush for larger areas working from the top down. Do not overload the brush with paint as it is better to apply two thin coats than one thick one. Allow plenty of drying time between coats – ideally leave them overnight.

Tip: Check your cupboard doors are suitable for painting by testing a small and inconspicuous area first. As a guide, unpainted solid wood doors are suitable for all satin and gloss wood paints although they need priming first with undercoat. For MDF, melamine and wood veneer it is important to choose a specialist door paint – many of which do not require priming first.

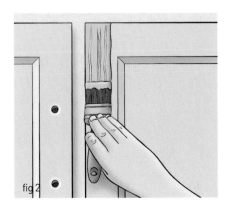

orange

THIS SHOWSTOPPER HAS HIDDEN DEPTHS – PALER APRICOT TONES CAN ADD A SOPHISTICATED EDGE WHILE BURNISHED TERRACOTTA MAKES AN ELEGANT ALTERNATIVE TO RED

Orange has an intensity that makes it impossible to ignore – whether it is being used to stop traffic or to decorate a room. But it can offer much subtler effects if you opt for a paler apricot shade or choose the rich tones of terracotta. In between are bold shades that work best on accessories or to define a bold feature wall. This is a colour that conjures up Mediterranean and tropical climates and its ability to add cheerful warmth makes it a great shade for brightening working rooms such as kitchens and offices. Richer and more intense tones can set an after-dark mood in dining areas or dramatic Eastern-style bedrooms, particularly if you add in red or gold accents.

Right **Rich tones of orange create an unusual and dramatic backdrop in a large open plan living and dining area. Accents of white on woodwork help to frame the divide between rooms**

why choose orange?

Orange adds warmth without sapping the light from a room, and this is a quality that can make it a better choice than red in some situations. It is also a good foil to darker brown shades, which is why it is such an excellent partner to dark furniture and rustic pine. Bold oranges can be a little too intense for many situations if you use them on all four walls. But partner them with a paler shade or use bold orange to define a feature wall or create a focal point through accessories and you are guaranteed a stimulating and inviting setting. Paler tones of apricot are well worth considering for bedrooms and country living areas, adding a burnished quality that works well with golds and neutrals. And if you want to capture the magic of the Mediterranean, look to rustic burnt oranges – especially suited to intimate dining rooms and traditional farmhouse kitchens.

Above **Rich orange can be partnered with paler shades. Here dark and light colours are used on facing walls to create a stimulating working environment**

Left **Soft apricot makes a good alternative to pink or lilac in a girl's bedroom – especially when you add in fairytale accessories such as this gold and white voile canopy**

soft apricot

Soft pale oranges have a similar quality to pale yellow – except that the temperature is turned up a notch. That makes them a good option if you want to add warmth without making a bold statement. Here are three ways to use apricot.

children's rooms
Apricot can be a good alternative to lilacs and pinks, especially if you want a colour that is not so overtly sugary or you are looking for a scheme that will not be overpowered by dark bedroom furniture. Add a voile canopy over the bed and fairytale accessories and this can be a feminine setting, particularly if you introduce touches of gold and red. This is also a shade that is easy to adapt by switching bedlinen and accessories around – a practical consideration if you are decorating a teenage bedroom.

romantic settings
Like peach, apricot has an opulent quality that can make it a perfect backdrop to romantic bedrooms with a distinctly French feel. It looks effective on floral wallpapers

where it adds a more sophisticated edge than yellow or pink, particularly when it is accessorized with heavy fabrics in shades of gold and burnt orange. Add in accents in rich creams and deeper shades of copper and terracotta.

classic living areas
Combined with creams and softer beiges, apricot makes a good choice for a traditional living room. You can use it on chintz fabrics without making the room appear too feminine – especially when you combine it with fern greens. Look for a pale almost neutral shade for walls and then add more warmth by using bolder patterns on curtains and cushions. Keep flooring neutral beige or cream if you want the overall effect to be light, or introduce dark stained floorboards and deep pile rugs if you want a cosier and more masculine effect.

Above **This opulent bedroom combines floral wallpaper in soft tones of apricot with richer gold and burnt orange on the heavy silk bedlinen and drapes**

Left **Chintz curtains add warmth to this traditional living room, making good partners to leaf greens and autumnal browns, as well as paler shades of cream**

create textured walls

You can create your own textured wallpaper effects on a feature wall using a simple combing technique. It is best to work with two toning shades of the same colour – in this case orange – and you need to start by painting the walls in your base colour. The combing effect is created by mixing paint with acrylic scumble, giving you time to work up the effect before the paint dries.

Left Textured walls are a good way to add depth and interest to a bold orange scheme and you can replicate wallpaper effects using a simple paint effect

parts scumble. Add less scumble if you want a denser effect, but remember this will make the paint dry quicker (experiment first on a piece of card to get the effect you want). Mix up enough of this mixture to cover the whole wall if possible. If not, measure the quantities so you can replicate the recipe (fig 1).

③ Using the paintbrush roughly paint the emulsion/scumble mix across the first strip of wall (fig 2).

④ Now run the rubber comb along the wall to produce the combed effect. Work quickly in a smooth motion from left to right to ensure an unbroken effect. Complete each strip before starting on the next one (fig 3).

⑤ Leave wall to dry overnight and then seal with an acrylic matt varnish.

YOU WILL NEED:

- **Vinyl matt emulsion in toning shades of orange**
- **Paint roller or pad**
- **Acrylic scumble**
- **Large paint tray or tin**
- **Paintbrush**
- **Rubber comb**
- **Acrylic matt varnish**

① Start by painting the wall in your base colour using a paint roller or pad. Leave to dry for at least eight hours.

② Mix up the second shade of orange with acrylic scumble in a paint tray or tin. Mix this thoroughly using a stick or paintbrush. The quantities you need depend on the effect you want, but as a rough guide go for one part paint to six

fig 1

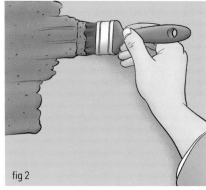

fig 2

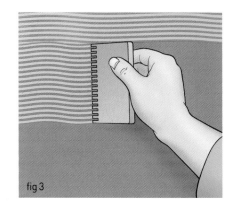

fig 3

bold orange

Stronger orange shades are great for feature walls, but they do not need to be restricted to the office or kitchen – you will find they set the scene equally well in a contemporary living room or atmospheric dining room. Here are four ways to use them around your home.

home offices
Orange is a naturally stimulating colour – which is why you so often see it in public spaces such as libraries and offices. At home it can be a useful colour for defining a working zone, particularly if you are furnishing it with contemporary grey metal. A flash of orange on one wall, or on flooring and accessories, warms up these chilly colours and creates a feeling of optimism. Choose a shade with hints of red/pink in it to soften the effect and add in plenty of white on facing walls to stop it from becoming oppressive.

contemporary living rooms
Spicy oranges make good partners to rich neutrals such as chocolate brown, and you can also add in metallic elements such as copper and gold to create an earthy setting in a living area. Choose orange for one or two walls only and add in plenty of white or cream on facing walls and furniture. Natural weave flooring such as coir or sisal adds texture and comfort underfoot and stops the setting from appearing too stark. Also introduce comfort zone features such as textured woollen and woven fabrics on accessories such as cushions and throws.

Above right **Orange is a natural partner to grey and steel – adding warmth that takes the chill off these functional office pieces. Choose a shade with red in it, and add white on facing walls**

Right **Bitter and spicy shades of orange work well with earthier tones of chocolate brown, rich red and copper in a contemporary living room, particularly if you add in neutral cream furniture**

dining rooms

For eating and entertaining areas orange can be a more suitable alternative to red if you want warmth without too much formality. Bold orange walls are a natural partner to dark wood – be it period mahogany, rustic stained pine and oak or contemporary furniture – and you can create after-dark glamour by mixing it with red accents. Alternatively, go for a more relaxed Tuscan ambience by adding in paint effects on walls and accessories in sunshine yellows. Earthy tones work well on accessories too, so look for details in wood, leather or smoked glass. Keep some elements neutral – for instance by choosing white tableware and napkins.

Left **Orange makes a good alternative to red for dining areas. Here it is combined with dark wood furniture and more contemporary elements such as the abstract canvas on one wall**

 COLOUR TIP

MIX RICH ORANGE AND RED

Combining dramatic orange and red may sound like a recipe for disaster, but in fact these two intense colours sit alongside each other on the colour wheel making them harmonious shades. Balance the two colours and you will find both the red and the orange appear less intense. They make good partners in a dining area or living room – or even in a lavish Indian-style bedroom – provided you match the strength of the colours. If you want this to be a restful setting, add in more muted partners such as rich browns and fawns and also remember to limit pattern to one or two areas – for instance curtains and cushions. Ensure your flooring is simple – either a pale neutral shade or mid to dark brown wood.

Right **Orange and red are mixed with richer shades of brown to create a dramatic living room with a distinctly autumnal flavour**

diluting the impact

A little orange goes a long way and if you want to include it in a room scheme without letting it become the dominant feature you need to balance it with other colours. Here are three ways to mix it with other colours and create a scheme that works.

balance it with cream
Painting orange over part of your walls is a good way to add warmth, but you need to find the the right colour to dilute its effect. Cream works well because it has more warmth than white, creating a contrast without the stark and modern feel. This is a look that can sit especially well in country kitchens or hallways. In halls go for tongue-and-groove panelling in cream up to dado rail height and then paint orange above the woodwork. In kitchens balance your orange walls with a cream ceiling and cream-painted kitchen furniture.

choose a rainbow effect
Give orange some competition by mixing it with other strong elements on the colour wheel. It mixes beautifully with its opposite number blue, but also works well with its harmonious shades of red and

Above **This orange kitchen has plenty of warmth but the cream units add a feeling of light. Green accents – an almost contrast to orange – add points of focus and stop the wall colour from dominating the room**

farmhouse kitchens
If you have a large kitchen that is as much a social as a working zone then orange is a good colour for adding atmosphere. This is a hue that can hold its own against brown, so it stops wooden fitted kitchen units from dominating a room. And if you add in atmospheric lighting it can be transformed into a space for relaxed entertaining. Look for stone or terracotta floor tiles to add country credentials and, if you want a more contemporary feel, introduce reflective elements such as steel on appliances. Remember to choose an orange that you can live with – burnt orange and terracotta have a mellow almost neutral quality that allows you to include additional colours within your scheme more easily.

Right **A line of orange glass vases makes a striking foil to soft peach pink. Here it enhances the delicate gold tracery pattern in the wallpaper background and highlights the heavy gilt mirror frame**

yellow. This is an effect that can be too much to handle so it is best to restrict yourself to no more than two bold colours on walls and add in white as a dividing colour. Alternatively use orange to define an area and introduce other colours as smaller accents – striped rugs, graphic pictures or a bold arrangement of multicoloured check and plain cushions.

use orange as an accent

Orange makes a striking accent colour, particularly when it is mixed in with its colour wheel neighbours red and yellow. It looks particularly effective against rich neutrals such as chocolate brown and caramel, adding a zest that enhances the richness of these earthy shades and stops them from looking too dark. Alternatively, try it as a dramatic foil for paler apricot, peach pink and gold – a group of bold orange vases makes a striking focal point on a shelf or mantelpiece.

Right Clever use of orange creates depth and points of focus in a high ceilinged hallway. White is used to divide up the orange and bold accents of red, blue, yellow and violet add to the rainbow effect

 DECORATOR'S NOTE

ADDING STENCILLED EFFECTS

Combine red, pink and orange and you create a fabulous Indian-style setting. Here walls were painted in two shades of pink and then Indian style motifs were stencilled on at border height and randomly over the wall. The same random effects were added to the floorlength curtain, stencilled on using fabric paint. If you want a similar effect without stencilling, dye white muslin cotton curtains in vibrant shades of red, pink and orange and then hang them together to frame a window or drape a bed. You can add stencilled effects in gold to the fabric, or stamp them if you want a simpler method. (For stencilling techniques, see pages 74 and 88. For stamping techniques, see page 52.)

Left Motifs stencilled onto both walls and curtain create a lavish Indian-style setting. A bolder stencilled border is picked out in red and orange halfway down the wall

create a rainbow effect with dye

Fabric dyes are a quick and inexpensive way to introduce the colours of the rainbow into your home through accessories. Plain white towels, curtains and bedlinen can be transformed into tropical hues of orange, pink and yellow to create accents for a hot tropical room scheme.

Before you start weigh the linen you want to dye. As a guide one pack of machine dye is usually enough to dye one bath towel or three hand towels (approximately 500g/1lb in dry weight). If you need more, increase the amount of dye and keep the quantity of salt the same.

Right **Tropical hues of orange, sunshine yellow and hot cerise turn towels into a striking focal point. It is easy to create these rainbow effects using machine dye and plain white cotton fabric**

YOU WILL NEED:
- **Plain white cotton towels, bedlinen or curtains**
- **Machine Dye**
- **500 g (1 lb) salt to fix the dye**

① Wash the linen you are dyeing and remove while damp.

② Dry the inside of the washing machine drum with a towel or cloth. Now put the dye into the bottom of the drum. Cover this with the salt then add your linen to the machine.

③ Set the machine on 60°C cotton cycle (no pre-wash) and allow the cycle to run its course.

④ Once the dye cycle has finished leave the linen inside the machine, add washing powder to the powder compartment and wash on the hottest (95°C) cycle to ensure excess dye is removed from the linen and the washing machine drum is cleaned.

⑤ Dry the linen out of direct sunlight and and away from strong heat to maintain the intensity of the colours.

Tips
- This technique works best on plain white or off white cotton. Pastel cotton can also be dyed but go for a deeper shade of the same colour.
- Do not overload the machine – the dye works most efficiently if you dye no more than a half-load at a time.

 DECORATOR'S NOTE

Mix and match towels or linen for best effect. You could combine a mid orange with a darker terracotta shade or mix bright red with hot pink. Match your dye packs just as if you were working with a paint chart.

Left **Bright pink and red make a great combination in a tropical room scheme**

index

acknowledgements

PICTURE CREDITS

The author and publisher would like to thank the following for permission to reproduce their images:

Aga (www.aga-rayburn.co.uk) p99 (b), 123 (t); AM.PM (www.redoute.co.uk) p50 (t); Anna French (www.annafrench.co.uk) p4-5 (c); Barker and Stonehouse (www.barker-stonehouse.co.uk) p107 (t); Bhs (www.bhs.co.uk) p50 (b), 121 (b); Brintons (www.brintons.net) p12 (br), 15 (t), 27 (bl), 33, 36, 37 (tl & tr), 47 (tl), 51 (r), 62 (b), 79 (r), 83 (r), 85 (t), 98 (b), 99 (t), 101 (t); Crown (www.crownpaint.co.uk) p10, 11,12 (t & bl), 16, 38 (l), 41, 44 (b), 60 (t), 61 (t), 67, 68 (t), 69 (t), 72 (br), 73, 80, 82 (b), 83 (l), 86 (t), 93, 95, 110, 113 (b), 115, 117, 124 (t); Crown Imperial (www.crown-imperial.co.uk) p26 (b), 63, 107 (b); Cuprinol (www.cuprinol.co.uk) p39; CWV (www.wallpapers-uk.com) p4 (l), 25 (t), 46 (l), 64 (t & b), 71 (b), 78; Debenhams (www.debenhams.com) front cover, p46 (br), 62 (t), 98 (t), 101 (b), 123 (b); Dulux (www.dulux.co.uk) p31, 48, 81, 94 (b), 108 (b), 112 (t), 114 (t), 118 (t), 122 (t); Dylon (www.dylon.co.uk) p125; Elgin & Hall (www.elgin.co.uk) p111; The English Stamp Company (www.englishstamp.com) p52, 53; Fired Earth (www.firedearth.co.uk) back cover (br), p6, 23, 100, 106, 108 (t); Focus (www.focusdiy.co.uk) back cover (tr), p72 (bl), 82 (t), 84, 100, 112 (b), 113 (t); Graham & Brown (www.grahambrown.com) p24 (t); Harlequin (www.harlequin.uk.com) back cover (bl), p1, 2, 7 (tr & bl), 32 (t), 40 (b), 43, 45, 55, 61 (b), 65 (b), 91, 109 (t), 120, 122 (b); Henny Donovan Motif (www.hennydonovanmotif.co.uk) p85 (b), 89, 102, 103, 124 (b); Homebase (www.homebase.co.uk) p59, 72 (t); IKEA (www.ikea.com) p118 (b); Jim Lawrence (www.jim-lawrence.co.uk) p17 (tl), 114 (b); John Lewis (www.johnlewis.com) p7 (c), 25 (b), 37 (b), 47 (b), 68 (b), 79 (l), 86 (b), 121 (t); Laura Ashley (www.lauraashley.com) p5 (l), 9, 17 (tr), 35, 51 (l), 56, 77, 87, 119 (t); Magnet (www.magnet.co.uk) p32 (b), 34 (t), 44 (t), 105; Oka (www.okadirect.com) p21, 38 (r), 40 (t), 92; Paint Quality Institute (www.paintquality.co.uk) p75, 96; Peacock Blue (www.peacockblue.co.uk) p27 (br); Plasti-kote (www.plasti-kote.com) p60 (b); Polycell (www.polycell.co.uk) p25 (b); Readyroll (HA Interiors) (www.hainteriors.com) p22 (t), 70; Roger Oates (www.rogeroates.co.uk) p26 (t), 34 (b); Romo Fabrics (www.romofabrics.com) p5 (r), 7 (br), 15 (b), 19, 20, 27 (c), 29, 30, 69 (b); Ronseal (www.ronseal.co.uk) p22 (b), 49; Sanderson (www.sandersonfabrics.co.uk) p97 (l), 109 (b), 119 (b); Wilman Interiors (www.wilman.co.uk) p57, 71 (t), 97 (r).